The Reminiscences of

Captain James R. Ogden

U. S. Navy (Retired)

U. S. Naval Institute
Annapolis, Maryland
1982

Preface

This oral history had an unusual origin. It grew out of the fact that the interviewer was also the editor of Air Raid: Pearl Harbor!, a book containing a collection of firsthand memories of the Japanese attack in 1941. Captain Ogden telephoned one day to register a mild protest to the time of birth given in the book for Admiral Thomas Moorer's first child. Later he called again, this time with a more substantive objection--that Admiral Moorer claimed to have made the first PBY patrol flight out of Pearl Harbor on 7 December 1941. Captain Ogden said the honor belonged to him rather than to his friend and classmate, Admiral Moorer.

As a consequence, Captain Ogden was invited to set the record straight and in the process to tell of his considerable naval aviation experience in addition to the Pearl Harbor episode. The memoir which emerged is a detailed look at PBYs in operation from 1938 to the Guadalcanal campaign in late 1942. In the meantime, Captain Ogden provides a dramatic account of his activities at Pearl Harbor and later at Midway. Subsequently, he was involved in flight training at Pensacola, commanded the seaplane tender Floyds Bay, and served in the carrier Philippine Sea when Rear Admiral Richard Byrd used her for a postwar exploration trip to Antarctica. The heart of the narrative, however, deals with the PBY, and in that regard it is probably the most thorough in the Naval Institute's oral history collection.

Unfortunately, Captain Ogden did not live to see the publication of his oral history, but he did contribute substantially to the final version, including making many changes to improve the accuracy and clarity of the final transcript. He died of a heart attack on 5 October 1982, not long after approving the last corrections. After he had already suffered one heart attack, he said to the interviewer during the final meeting to go over transcript changes, "I guess we finished this just in time." Indeed we did, and the source materials of naval history are thus richer because Captain Ogden made the following narrative available. It stands as a memorial to his own fine career and provides increased understanding of the valuable role the PBY played in the U.S. Navy.

Paul Stillwell
Director of Oral History
U.S. Naval Institute
December 1982

Biography of Captain James R. Ogden, USN (Ret.), 72383/1310

June 1928 -- Enlisted in U.S. Navy. Basic training and Naval Academy Preparatory Class, Norfolk, Virginia.

1929-1933 -- Midshipman at U.S. Naval Academy, Annapolis, Maryland.

1933-1935 -- Served in heavy cruiser Chicago (CA-29) as ensign under instruction.

1935-1936 -- Completed flight training at Pensacola, Florida. Designated Naval Aviator, promoted to lieutenant (junior grade)

1936-1938 -- Attached to aviation unit of heavy cruiser Northampton (CA-26).

1938-1939 -- Assigned to VP-7, a PBY squadron based at San Diego, California. Participated in mass non-stop flight from San Diego to Coco Solo, Canal Zone.

1939-1942 -- Assigned to VP-23 in Hawaii, promoted to lieutenant. Present in Pearl Harbor on 7 December 1941. Participated in Battle of Midway. Squadron operated in support of landings at Guadalcanal. Became commanding officer in August 1942, promoted to lieutenant commander.

1943-1944 -- Stationed at Naval Air Training Command, Pensacola, Florida, as commanding officer of instrument squadron and on staff, Chief of Naval Air Training; promoted to commander.

1945-1946 -- Commissioned seaplane tender Floyds Bay (AVP-40) as first commanding officer.

1946-1947 -- Navigator of carrier Philippine Sea (CV-47). Participated in Operation Highjump (Antarctic).

1947-1950 -- Served in the Bureau of Aeronautics, Washington, D.C.

1950-1952 -- Served in Headquarters, Atlantic Division, Military Air Transport Service at Westover Air Force Base, Massachusetts. Promoted to rank of captain.

1952 -- Ordered to duty under instruction at the Naval War College, Newport, Rhode Island.

1953 -- Ordered to duty on the faculty of the Armed Forces Staff College, Norfolk, Virginia.

1955-1957 -- Served as chief of staff for Commander Carrier Division 15, embarked in the USS Boxer (CV-21).

1957-1958 -- Deputy Director, Aviation Training Division, office of the Chief of Naval Operations, Washington, D.C.

1958-1959 -- Deputy Chief of Staff, Headquarters, U.S. Taiwan Defense Command, Military Assistance Advisory Group, Taipei, Taiwan.

1959-1960 -- Director, Navy Recruiting, Second Navy Recruiting Area, Baltimore, Maryland. Retired 30 June 1960.

1960-1972 -- Taught mathematics at Severn School, Severna Park, Maryland.

Decorations -- Air Medal for flights in Central and South Pacific, 1941-1942. American Defense, Asiatic Pacific Theater with three stars; American Theater; World War II Victory Medal; Occupation (Japan); China Service; National Defense Service Medal; Korean Service Medal.

Captain Ogden is married to the former Mary Elizabeth (Betty) King of Annapolis, Maryland. They have two children, daughter Elizabeth Ann and son Richard William II (Naval Academy, class of 1966). Captain and Mrs. Ogden live at 236 Puritan Place, Annapolis, Maryland 21401.

DECLARATION OF TRUST

The undersigned does hereby appoint and designate as his (her) Trustee herein, the Secretary-Treasurer and Publisher of the United States Naval Institute to perform and discharge the following duties, powers, and privileges in connection with the possession and use of a certain taped interview between the undersigned and the Oral History Department of the United States Naval Institute.

1. Classification of Transcript.

   (X)a. If classified OPEN, the transcript(s) may be read or the recording(s) audited by the qualified personnel upon presentation of proper credentials, as determined by the Secretary-Treasurer of the U.S. Naval Institute.

   ( )b. If classified PERMISSION REQUIRED TO CITE OR QUOTE, the user will be required to obtain permission in writing from the interviewee prior to quoting or citing from either the transcript(s) or the recording(s).

   ( )c. If classified PERMISSION REQUIRED, permission must be obtained in writing from the interviewee before the transcribed interview(s) can be examined or the tape recording(s) audited.

   ( )d. If classified CLOSED, the transcribed interview(s) and the tape recording(s) will be sealed until a time specified by the interviewee. This may be until the death of the interviewee or for any specified number of years.

2. It is expressly understood that in giving this authorization, I am in no way precluded from placing such restrictions as I may desire upon use of the interview at any time during my lifetime, nor does this authorization in any way affect my rights to the copyright of my literary expressions that may be contained in the interview.

Witness my hand and seal this 9th day of July 1982

James R. Ogden

I hereby accept and consent to the foregoing Declaration of Trust and the powers therein conferred upon me as Trustee:

Interview No. 1 with Captain James R. Ogden

Place: His home in Annapolis, Maryland

Date: March 10, 1982

Subject: His experiences serving in PBY patrol planes

By: Paul Stillwell

Q: Captain, could you please start out by giving us some background and description on the PBY itself?

Capt. O.: Fine. The PBY was slow, sturdy, dependable, versatile, easy to fly and maintain. It's a seagoing first cousin of the DC-3 (also called the R4D, C-47, and a Gooney Bird). There are some in use today, as you can see from the beer commercials. Our gas tanks were built into the wings, unfortunately with plates so that people could inspect the interior from time to time, which I, as one of the smallest people in the squadron, had the necessity to do. They held 1,200-plus gallons. On occasion we'd put them down the ramp so we could really fill them up to capacity. Later on, as the war approached, we cut down on their capacity somewhat by installation of self-sealing tanks on the inside.

The landing characteristics -- we had two ways of landing. In smooth water, the fly-on landing about 70 or 75 knots, a rough-water landing technique of a full stall. Tom Moorer reports a completely different type of landing operation in which all of the trailing edges are burned off the wings, both fuel tanks on fire, shot up and was able to make a swim-away landing downwind at 120 knots--not recommended for usual procedures. They were seaworthy when operating as boats after they went down at sea; they were sturdy enough to stand open-sea landings and takeoffs. Single engine operation was fair.

The crew composition and their stations--we would normally fly with three pilots; the plane commander and the first pilot in the seats with the flight controls available to either or both. The third pilot was navigator and possibly also manned the forward turret where a .30-caliber machine gun was mounted and where the bombsight was. The bombsight could be cut in to make a completely controlled bombing run, automatically controlled, and also was therefore able to function as an automatic pilot for long flights.

Q: How did you determine who filled the three slots of pilot and copilot and navigator? Was that strictly by seniority?

Capt. O.: Well, partly by seniority and partly by experience. Actually, some of our best patrol plane commanders were enlisted naval aviation pilots. They stayed with us longer, and they were among the most reliable that we had. At Midway in two of the three basic sectors that we covered, I had put in two of these former enlisted pilots who had later been commissioned. So it wasn't a question of seniority in terms of rank, but seniority in terms of experience. When not in that forward station, the third pilot would man the navigation table. Actually, if we were on a training mission, the pilots would rotate from one position to another, perhaps. But normally the patrol plane commander would stay in one of the control seats. The navigation table was in the compartment immediately aft of the pilots with the navigator on the port side and the radioman on the starboard side. The pilots had voice transmission for reasonably short range, but the radioman operated with key transmissions and used a trailing antenna that could be put out and down in such a way that it could be adjusted to the frequencies that were being used at the time. The plane crew chief, aviation mechanic, was the tower, in the pylon which connected the wings to the main body and it was from there that he controlled gasoline flow, checked the tanks, and operated the wing-tip floats which were retractable after flying. Immediately aft of the navigation table and the radio table were bunks. They were pull-down bunks, double bunks for four people. Immediately after that section was where the two blisters, one on either side, where the two entry places were. We mounted .50-caliber machine guns on each of those. These positiosn were also manned for use of sea anchors when we made approaches to the ramp or buoy after landing. The PBY had no water rudder, so steering was primarily by use of either engine. The sea anchors, on one side or the other, provided additional steering when strong cross winds occurred and also slowed approaches for easier handling by beaching crews.

Q: Did the blister open up so you could trail an anchor out of it?

Capt.O.: Yes, that's right. Originally, the PBY-2s and 3s that we had in the first place just had a sliding door hatch that we'd push forward out of the way and you would lean out, but the 5s when they came out just before the war had actual Plexiglas blisters that protected the people because these were used as lookout posts when we were patrolling.

Q: Did the blister then slide so you could open it up?

Capt. O.: Yes. It was a canopy type thing.

Q: How did the pilot communicate with the people to tell them to trail the anchor?

Capt. O.: There was an intercom system so you could talk with all of the stations that I mentioned. Further back, there was a tunnel hatch which had a .30-caliber machine gun, but could obviously only shoot down and this hatch also served for many purposes. We would use that to drop flares or smoke bombs to check the wind direction and to mark things in the water. The head was back there for obvious reasons. This position has also been known to be an ideal fishing post for advanced base operations.

The maintenance and logistics--each crew had presumably a crew chief who was usually either a chief petty officer or a first class petty officer and a radioman, sometimes an ordnanceman, and at least another mech [mechanic]. These were the crews that would fly the planes and they stayed on the plane virtually all the time. The pilots might shift from time to time and fly different planes. There was an assigned crew for each plane and when we went into squadron formation, they were in appropriate position-- that is, the skipper would fly number one and the exec in number seven and so forth. But the crew almost invariably stayed with the plane, and they were responsible for all of the daily routine upkeep, cleanliness, and everything else for the plane. There were squadron maintenance crews that handled major checks.

Q: They were assigned to individual planes?

Capt. O.: They were not assigned to any individual planes. They made major structural repairs.

Q: Who would do the changing of engines?

Capt. O.: That was done with the squadron, the change of engines, structural repairs, major checks where we did a tune-up, so to speak. And of course the squadron also had a radio shack and we had an ordnance crew. When the guns weren't in the planes, they were in the hangars in the places where the squadron ordnance was to take care of them.

Shore based, we also had required beaching crews. The PBY, when brought up the ramp, required two very cumbersome, heavy landing wheels that required detaching. The tires were big enough so that they would float, but it was a problem that required several people on each side to handle this gear, and it required tractors with long lines to let them down the ramp to haul them into place and to let them down the ramp and to recover them on return. The fueling ashore was, as a general rule, by gas trucks. Some places had built-in fueling systems where it could be done with a hose from various stations.

The launching and recovery times--when we were trying to get things out in a hurry, we could probably launch a plane in five minutes or perhaps a little bit less. Recovery would take somewhat longer because of the need to make slow approaches and it was a little awkward getting the plane turned around sideways so that it went back up the ramp tail first.

For tender support, we had different kinds. In Patrol Wing 1 the only large tender we had was the Wright, a converted something I'm not sure what, but obviously it wasn't built as a seaplane tender. Later, in Pat Wing 2, we had the Curtiss which was built for that purpose, and it had something that the Wright did not have: a capability to take a plane or sometimes more than one plane aboard at a time with special cranes. Again, in Patrol Wing 1 we had some smaller tenders: two old four-pipe destroyers converted to two pipes with the other engine room spaces made available to handle seaplanes; and also a couple of the Swan-class fleet tugs which were very slightly modified to be able to give gasoline, and that was about the only function they really performed. They were helpful for a single transit plane going through to somewhere else, or they could take a few planes for overnights or maybe a couple of days so we could get into places. But obviously, they had to be positioned ahead of time.

Q: They were fairly small ships. They wouldn't have a large gasoline supply either, would they?

Capt. O.: No. That's why I say they were only used for small operations. You asked that I talk about the transition from the cruiser seaplane that I had to the PBYs. Perhaps a little chronological idea of how this went along--first, I guess, I should say that I reported on May 31st of 1938 to Commander of Patrol

Wing 1 who was at that time, and throughout my tour there, Marc Mitscher.

Q: This was based where?

Capt. O.: In San Diego. The squadron was VP-7. We had four squadrons there: 7, 9, 11, and 12. My squadron commander throughout was S. B. Moore of '21. Frank Ward was the exec.

Q: And when you say '21, you mean the Class of '21 [at the U.S. Naval Academy].

Capt. O.: Class of '21. I'm giving that because at this stage of the game, practically all of the senior officers were Academy graduates and this helps to place their approximate seniority.

Q: And you were a lieutenant (junior grade) at the time?

Capt. O.: Yes. The skipper and exec were lieutenant commanders. There were perhaps four lieutenants and three JGs (all classmates).

Q: Who were your classmates in that squadron?

Capt. O.: Charley Robertson (C. E. Robertson) and Bill Shafer. The remaining pilots were aviation cadets and most of these were from the very first classes of the aviation cadets. I went through Pensacola in Class 80, and the first cadets were in Class 81. (Incidentally, one of my classmates in 80 was John Sidney McCain, Sr., and I had the distinction of having his left leg when we threw him in Pensacola Bay after his solo. As I pointed out, we also had aviation pilots, one of whom at that time was assigned to one of the planes as a patrol plane commander.)

Q: The aviation pilots were the enlisted men?

Capt. O.: Yes, the enlisted men. One of the aviation cadets was a very capable fellow, Henry Bridgers, whom I ran into later at Pensacola, and he was largely responsible for a completely new way to conduct instrument training. I took the instrument squadron and worked in the development of this program there and later went to the staff where Henry was with me. Then he and another member of his group wrote the book which is still current, the Instrument Training Manual.

As for my transition to flying a PBY, at Pensacola our first two basic squadrons were seaplanes (where we all soloed) and then the landplane trainers. But in squadron 3 we flew the scout plane, a two-seat type of plane on wheels. In squadron 4, we flew in patrol planes and torpedo planes, again water based. Squadron 5 was in fighters, so that our training was universal and not specialized as it later got to be. So we had some patrol plane experience. I was very fortunate in going through my patrol plane experience at Pensacola. These planes were far from being as easy to fly as the PBYs, and I was happy to have Tom Moorer as my co-student, because he was stronger than I was and sometimes it was needed. I reported to my first flight in VP-7 on the 6th of June and on the 6th of July and 25 flight hours later, I was accepted as a qualified patrol plane commander.

Q: You say you first flew on the 6th of June and on the 6th of July you were qualified?

Capt. O.: I then qualified and that 25 hours included the nine hours when we flew from San Diego to Seattle.

Q: How did you come to get into this squadron? Had you requested patrol planes?

Capt. O.: No, I had not. Before I went to Pensacola, I had been appointed as aviation gunnery observer for my last six months of the two years I had on the Chicago. We rode the rear seat and spotted for ship's gunfire. When I left Pensacola, I requested cruiser duty partly because I had had experience and partly because this type of duty seemed inevitable and I wanted to get it out of the way so I could go on to something else and not have that interrupt my later program. I went to the Northampton for two years immediately before going to VP-7. But I did not request duty in patrol planes.

Q: This is just where the Bureau of Navigation had you go?

Capt. O.: This is where Adolphus Andrews sent me. His name appears just about as much on my orders as Marc Mitscher's does at the bottom.

Q: So if you had had patrol plane training at Pensacola, then there probably wasn't much of a transition to go through.

Capt. O.: Not really that much, just in terms of flying the airplane.

Q: So really only 25 hours from what you said.

Capt. O.: Yes. And fortunately this was enough because I assure you that on the 7th of July, we took off from Sand Point in Seattle for Kodiak for one of the hairiest flights that I've ever had in my life. We were going in squadron formation, which seemed to be the way to go in those days, and as we cut straight across the North Pacific on the way to Kodiak, the squadron was trying to fly over whatever weather we got into. In spite of the fact that this was July, eventually we got high enough that we got in a real good snow storm and then things started happening--the windshield iced over and things got a little bit hairy. Fortunately the squadron had a doctrine for going from formation to individual flights and being in number 11, the tail-end Charlie, it was no problem for me to turn around and go back in the opposite direction, which I did for long enough to make sure that everybody else was far enough away so I could go back to course. So the rest of the flight was single, but in the meantime, apparently my oil cooler had also iced over and the oil temperature was going up and the oil pressure was going down, so that we started breaking out life jackets and whatnot with not a very pleasant prospect. Fortunately when we got back down a little bit lower, the ice melted and we were able to make it in.

Q: What did you use for navigation in a situation like that?

Capt. O.: We had a prediction of what the winds were. We had a capability of getting radio bearings on the tender. They would send us what we called MOs, homing signals, just a signal, "M"

Ogden #1 -11

being two dashes and "O" being three dashes, a more or less steady thing that we could identify and home in on. Otherwise, in weather like that, you're on dead reckoning.

Q: So mainly it was dead reckoning as opposed to instrument navigation?

Capt. O.: Obviously we had magnetic compasses and we had directional gyros. We could do a reasonably good job. This was something in the order of an 11- or 12- hour flight, I believe. The navigation seemed to work out all right.

Q: And you compensated for the predicted winds?

Capt. O.: Yes. Then we could take a drift sight. When there were breaks in the clouds and we could see anything, we would drop a float out and when it hit the water, it would give you some smoke and then you had a gadget to give you bearings and you saw whether the bearing was straight or if it went off to one side or another and you could tell how much you were drifting from one side to another.

Q: Did you use celestial any on long flights?

Capt. O.: Yes, we did have bubble octants that we could use. They were helpful; it kept you in the ball park but was not exactly pinpoint navigation. But it was something in which we were trained and had the equipment to do, celestial navigation.

From Kodiak, we were to go to Sitka. Because things were pretty cloudy and we had had our experience about going on top, we decided that we should go under the thing. This is a six-hour flight. We were in a tight squadron Big V*. I was number 11, tail end of six planes and I could always see the plane immediately ahead of me and sometimes I could see the second one ahead. I don't remember that I, as the high man, was ever over 300 feet and I felt that at times the skipper must be taxiing rather than flying, but we managed to do about six hours of this before arriving safely at Sitka. We had four squadrons on this operation. Two squadrons went to Kodiak first, and the other two went to Sitka. Then on the day that we flew to Sitka, the Sitka planes flew to Kodiak and they were on top of everything, very clear, and managed to have it clear when they got there, so they didn't have any problem with coming down. Really got the worst of it both ways. We finally got back to San Diego about 1 August. From the 9th to the 12th of August, the whole wing was involved with a fleet tactical problem that was going on and it was during this exercise that my friend and often skipper [Marc Mitscher] pulled one of the most heroic peacetime ploys I've had the fortune to listen in on.

The operation problem that we were having was being conducted by Commander Scouting Force [Vice] Admiral Adolphus Andrews. Our function, if I remember it, was primarily squadron formations for night bombing. Fortunately we never had to use any of these tactics in actual operation. All four squadrons from San Diego were out operating, not in a four-squadron formation, but each squadron in formation, and all 48 airplanes, as far as I know, as many as

---

*Like a flock of geese, in more ways than one.

we had available, were out. When we started getting reports that they expected San Diego to fog in very shortly, this was a critical situation as far as we were concerned, because this happens very rapidly and once it did, there was no way we could get into San Diego. Long Beach would probably be doing the same thing, so we were considering the prospect of having to fly over the mountins and then to the Salton Sea which was our only alternate location --which nobody was very happy about doing at midnight without any preparation, particularly with 48 airplanes. So Marc Mitscher called up the boss and explained the situation and said we requested permission to return to base. Reply: "Remain on station."

Q: This is from Admiral Andrews?

Capt. O.: Yes. A little bit later: "Consider it urgent that we return to base as soon as possible."
 Reply: "Remain on station."
 Next transmission: "Unless otherwise directed, am returning to base." Click--with the radio going off loud and clearly.

Q: So there was no way he could be otherwise directed.

Capt. O.: He could not be otherwise directed.

Q: When did that incident take place, approximately?

Capt. O.: This was during these fleet exercises in the early part of August. All of these dates are 1938. We managed to survive that operation. We did get back and the fog did set in and we were just in time. It was really helpful.

Ogden #1 -14

Q: So Mitscher had a better appreciation of it than Andrews did.

Capt. O.: Yes. Well, Mitscher was an old-time pilot, and it was his business and he had to do what he knew had to be done or we would have had real problems.

The program for the rest of 1938 would show you approximately the kind of operations that patrol planes used in those days. Remember that we were at San Diego and there was little need or opportunity to conduct long-range searches for practice, because there was nothing to look for and we had other things to do for training. Roughly, in August and September, we engaged in gunnery practice and bombing. In October, we did something which very few PBY squadrons had the opportunity to do, as far as I know. That was torpedo practice which included, at the end, a record drop and each pilot and his squadron, as far as I know, (and certainly I did), had a drop.

Q: It's interesting you say that you didn't need practice in searchi but that's the way those planes were primarily used during the war.

Capt. O.: When we got to Pearl later, it was a completely different situation. I am referring to the way Patrol Wing 1 operated. In Patrol Wing 1 we were in formation almost more than we operated as single planes, because as we got into the next exercise, you can see again the accent on working with the fleet and supportin the fleet as a bombing part of our mission rather than the "B" as opposed to the "P," our designation.

Q: I'm saying, though, that in fact, the things that you practiced for most were used the least once the war came.

Capt. O.: As it so happened.

Q: Patrol Wing 10, for example, tried bombing in the Philippines with not very good results.

Capt. O.: I didn't realize that they had. We practiced bombing in Hawaii, but more as individual bombing than as squadron. In other words, this is the prime difference between the operation of Patrol Wing 2 as opposed to Patrol Wing 1. It was individual work. We did a certain amount of formation flying in Hawaii, but not extensively.

Q: It was good that you were in both so you can give us a comparison of the differences.

Capt. O.: In November, we worked on tactics and, again, this involved squadrons working with groups of planes. Most of December was in preparation for the trip to the East Coast. This, I'm sure, set a record for patrol planes of almost any type. On the 10th and 11th of January 1939, the 48 planes of Patrol Wing 1 made a mass flight from San Diego to Coco Solo [Panama Canal Zone], a distance of roughly 3,100 miles. My particular flight time was 26.4 hours.

Q: That's continuously in the air?

Capt. O.: Right. I say "right" and now I refer to the Wright which was at the Gulf of Fonseca [between El Salvador and Colombia].

This was about two-thirds of the way down, and she was stationed there and was used by perhaps four or five of the planes whose fuel consumption indicated that they probably wouldn't get all the way to Coco Solo. They stopped and refueled from the Wright and went on from there and joined us later. Some of those who did make it, I understand, ran out while taxiing in to the beach and some people made it on one engine. I had enough for perhaps another half hour or 20 minutes more when we got there.

The whole idea of the flight down was to participate in Fleet Problem XX. I'm giving the dates specifically to illustrate the fact that while we could fly in one day from San Diego to Coco Solo, our next flight to San Juan could not be made until the Wright had transited the canal and proceeded to San Juan (January 24th). Thus while our planes could have made the complete movement in three days, they were tied to a "slow boat" which required the better part of a month.

Q: What facilities were there for you at Coco Solo? There was an air station.

Capt. O.: Oh, yes. Coco Solo had a patrol wing down there, so they had the facilities to put us up. I say the facilities; we had more planes in our group, I'm sure. They didn't have more than two or three squadrons down in Coco Solo. We couldn't have operated out of Coco Solo, and with seven squadrons there was no way that that could be handled. Actually, the planes were out at buoys most of the time, as far as I know. So it was not until the 24th that we went to San Juan. And then it was not until the 27 of February that Fleet Problem XX took place. We were considerably more than a month in San Juan, with all 48 planes based on the <u>Wright</u>. This created not only the normal problem of having a tender which wasn't built as a tender trying to take care of as many people as we had along, but another problem came up which nobody had foreseen and we didn't even understand when we started off. Our planes were all at buoys at San Juan harbor and were very close to what became the first airfield down there, but it was also very close to a tenement district which was built on stilts out into the water. After we had been there for a couple of days and got squared away, we started to fly a little bit and we found that planes were very hard to get off the water and in some cases we couldn't even get them off. They found out that the high amount of sewage in the water was just exactly what a barnacle needed to thrive on, and we found out eventually that for this whole six-week period we were there, each plane had to be brought out on a Pan Am ramp at San Juan and have the barnacles scraped off before we could even fly. This explains the lack of flying that happened in the next month after we got to Norfolk (I have in my notes for this period: "Work on Planes." And that's exactly what we did for quite a while.)

Q: You said you were working on tactics during this period. Was this under the direction of Captain Mitscher?

Capt. O.: Yes, but it was called a fleet problem at this stage of the game. I was with the fleet when they went through the canal in 1934 as the fleet had exercises on the East Coast. How much of the fleet came from the Pacific through the canal I'm not sure.

Ogden #1 -18

I'm not sure whether we depended on only what was on the East Coast, which couldn't have been very much, but again, it was the same sort of a thing in which whatever we were doing was by squadrons.

Q: Was it more in the bombing and torpedoing or scouting during the problem?

Capt. O.: It was bombing and a good deal of it at night.

Q: How do you run a bombing problem at night? Can you describe that?

Capt. O.: We went through the motions, let's put it that way. I don't know whether it would have worked, whether it could possibly have worked, but it gave the fleet some small sense of security that somebody was going to be there helping them out. We could drop flares; the battleships could shoot star shells. There were ways to illuminate and presumably if you could see it, we could do as well. Our bombing was mostly what they called high-altitude bombing, around 9,000 or 10,000 feet, something like that. If you've got 48 planes flying and you hit the general area, something might happen, but I wouldn't say that it would really be that effect against ships any more than the B-17s were effective against ships where they had occasion to try to do that, although I have seen very, very, very precise Air Force B-17 bombings and results of B-17 bombings in Japan. I've seen a refinery built out in the Inland Sea that was utterly and completely destroyed and wooden shacks right alongside the perimeter that were untouched.

Ogden #1 -19-

Q: But that was probably daytime.

Capt. O.: Maybe and maybe not.

Q: Was your bombsight helpful on these night runs?

Capt. O.: Oh, we couldn't do a thing in the world without the bombsight. It was a good instrument. The bombsight operator corrected your pattern, he'd look through the site, and he'd set up whatever speed and direction they thought the target was making and he coached the pilot on until he got the sights, on where he wanted in the setup and then he would take over from the pilot at the last minute. Now, when we were doing squadron work or group work, only the leader controlled, and we made the drop in formation. He called the drop, and the whole squadron would drop it at once.

Q: So he called the drop over the radio and you'd go on his signal?

Capt. O.: Yes. I say we got to Norfolk in the early part of March and in the middle part of April we went to Newport, Rhode Island, for what I have listed in my log as a short Army-Navy exercise. I do not understand or remember exactly how the Army was concerned except that presumably there were some Army Air Corps planes involved in the operation. I do not have a distinct memory of this operation. But while at Newport, our orders were changed to have us return to San Diego as soon as possible for what particular reason I'm not in the position to know. While we were around in that area, many of us had received our orders detaching us from the squadron as soon as we got back. In any case, we were all looking forward --and of course I had my orders to go to Hawaii with several others in the squadron. So we left on 1 May, we left Norfolk and flew to Guantanamo, the next day to Coco Solo, and then we had to wait. In the meantime, I presume, the Wright had made tracks for Panama and therefore on 8 May instead of trying to fly all the way to San Diego nonstop, we flew into the Gulf of Fonseca where the Wright was and then refueled and took the rest of the trip back from Fonseca to San Diego.

Q: Was was the range of the PBYs?

Capt. O.: Well, the range of the PBY is roughly 3,130 miles, althoug this was by far the longest flight that I believe the PBY was ever required to make and as I say, later there were things that cut the range down even further. This flight required that we really examine very carefully the most gas-saving efficient way to fly. We left San Diego, and it was an experience being able to take off. The day we left, the water was glassy, which is hard for takeoff because we really need a little bit of a chop to get off. I know we were not the first one to take off, and I remember seeing some planes that had come all the way down from the destroyer base at San Diego and got all the way practically to Point Loma and never got off and had to turn around and go back and try it again. Part of it was knowing exactly how to load the plane and the distribution of the people and any heavy equipment inside the plane was one thing for an optimum takeoff run. Then you shifted things around once you got in the air. In other words, anybody that wasn't required to be at his station for takeoff would come up and either get all the way up in the bow or stand right in back of the pilots to have weight forward for better distribution for the takeoff and then you would go further back so we would fly at zero tab setting, in other words, so the plane balanced itself off later in the air. As we flew out of San Diego and were working up to the optimum altitude to fly for gas consumption, about 9,000 feet, we were probably all the way down to the southern tip of Baja, California, before we got to 9,000 feet and I'm sure not over 75 knots that whole time just because we had worked quite hard during that period of December trying to find out just how to make that work. In some cases it did and some planes and some engines were just a little more gas thirsty than others were, which is why we had the variation that we had.

Q: Was it considered a black mark against a pilot or crew if they couldn't get the plane off when most of the others could?

Capt. O.: I don't know. I had no problem. I would assume that the guy got the treatment from the squadron commander that if he was a ballplayer that he would have gotten from a manager for pulling some kind of a boo-boo like I read about in the paper this morning. Earl Weaver* was unhappy with one of his outfielders.

Q: Were the PBYs used much overland? I mean, theoretically you could have flown from the East Coast to the West Coast overland.

Capt. O.: I have often wondered about that because one of my classmates, Murray Hanson, had an article recently in Shipmate**--I was aware of it at the time--in which they tried to fly from San Diego

---

*Manager of the Baltimore Orioles.
**In two parts: March 1980, pages 27-30; April 1980, pages 23-26.

to Corpus Christi. Of course, unfortunately, I don't know why they encountered bad weather, because it seemed like a routine sort of operation that they might have waited, but in any case, they ended up landing in a "lake" in Texas which turned out to be mostly mud. It was quite an interesting thing. As a matter of fact, it wasn't really all that funny because people ended up bailing out, all except the two pilots who brought it in. One guy was lost in the bail-out, and then others were lost after they were picked up in somebody else's plane. But I never understood why a transcontinental all the way from San Diego to Norfolk wouldn' have been within the capabilities. I have several flights in my record of 20 hours or more and several more in over 19. There was no problem in flying 2,400 miles from either San Diego or Oaklan out to Hawaii or the reverse (except the PBY-5A, with retractable landing gear, needed extra tanks).

Q: Would you stay in the cockpit that whole period, or would you trade off and get some sleep?

Capt. O.: On the flight down to Coco Solo somewhat early in the flight and in the middle of the night, I got out of the seat and the squadron was all there in front of me and the lights and everything else that we could see. I turned it over to a cadet whom I will not name and said, "All right, let's keep her here," and I went back and got a bowl of soup or something and I came back up after 15 minutes and I looked around and said, "Where are they?"

He said, "I don't know." Well, what had happened is that all of the lights on the PBY were topside (which I didn't think about at the time), but now I know better. All I had to do was climb up a little bit and I would have found out where everybody else was. I didn't know that, so the next morning I got a glimpse of the morning sun shining off the rest of the squadron about 20 miles ahead. Needless to say, that 15 minutes was the only time that I was out of the seat on this particular flight. As I say, we could use the bombsight as an automatic pilot, but they didn't always work.

Q: How did your experience in that squadron wind up then, before you proceeded to your next duty?

Capt. O.: This was about it. Once we got back to San Diego, we were on the verge of being transferred. We had a little bit of leave and we sorted out our transportation. My wife had driven east during this time, and her brother came out and drove her back, but she didn't want to drive back out to the West Coast. So we arranged to have somebody take my car and drive out and we would pick up his car in San Diego and we all would meet on the dock in San Francisco instead of park on the ship.

The trip out was interesting because there were several people not only from Patrol Wing 1 but otherwise on the ship. We were fortunate enough to make the Matsonia instead of the originally scheduled Army transport.

Q: That was the Republic that you had mentioned to me?

Capt. O.: That I had originally been assigned to. Among the people who were there were Tom and Carrie Moorer, and my relationship with Tom and later with Carrie goes all the way back to the fact that we were in the same company at the Naval Academy. We were ordered to training in Pensacola in the same group; we flew a great deal of our time together there, and had one beautiful night formati flight which was interesting in that our instructor and the lead for the three-plane flight was Eddie Sanders* who was noted among the students for his wanting us to fly close, so Tom and I were flying wing on him, and we decided to satisfy his demand for that. So when we lined up on the runway just before dark, (we always took off in formation) Tom and I put our wings inside his tail and everything looked fine and we started off. As we got up about 15 feet, and he looked around to his left at Tom and then quickly looked around at me and we were right there where we had been when we lined up for the takeoffs. So he gestured to move back a little bit, move back a little bit. Well, we moved back about 6 inches, and then he apparently was trying to show us that we couldn't do that. What maneuvers we went through I haven't the foggiest idea, but I do remember having seen the lights of Pensacola from every conceivable angle that I could see. When we got back to the ramp, we taxied back and the whole group was standing out there looking and apparently had seen it and among others, was the squadron flight officer, Dave McDonald** (later CNO), and he beckoned Sanders into his office and they had a nice chat about how he should conduct his flying test.

Q: What kind of plane was this that you were flying?

---

*Lieutenant (junior grade) Eddie R. Sanders ('30).
** Lieutenant David L. McDonald, USN ('28).

Capt. O.: This was an F4B-4. This came up much later when at Tom's retirement ceremony I was invited along with practically all the rest of our class that was available. After the ceremony in the hangar at Andrews Air Force Base, they went out on the field and somebody landed and taxied up in an F4B-4 in front of all the assembled people, and just about that time the Blue Angels flew by in tight formation, so that when we went through the receiving line, I said, "Tom, does today remind you of anything?"

And he said, "It sure does--that flight down at Pensacola." So he remembered that one. In any case, we went out together.

Q: Can you recall other incidents? I'm sure you have a good store of them about Admiral Moorer.

Capt. O.: Oh, yes, I was going to get to that. We went out together on the Matsonia, we ended up in houses not too far apart, and we were very close throughout that entire period. We played bridge two or three times a week; we'd go down to the beach; Tom and I and some of the others would play golf at a country club several times a week. As a matter of fact, both Tom's wife, Carrie, and my wife, Betty, would accompany us around as part of their prenatal conditioning, and there was always the question about which hole our first born were going to arrive. His came about a month before ours. They were christened together, and so we were really close. Towards the end, Tom took his trip which he has explained down to the East Indies as preparation for the eventual arrival of the B-17s out in the Philippines.*

---

*See Air Raid: Pearl Harbor!, page 202-206.

Ogden #1 -26

Q: Where were your quarters there? Were they on Ford Island?

Capt. O.: No, we lived out in town. We were up in Alewa Heights. From my house, we could see Pearl Harbor. It was closer than most of the houses. Most everybody lived out in town. There were only very few quarters available on Ford Island. The field on Ford Island had been an Army field until Hickam was built, and they were still doing repair and maintenance work over there. When we first got there, the quarters were mostly occupied by the Army. The Navy moved in, and the squadron commanders were out there in definite quarters. But only a few of the other quarters were available and some people preferred to go there, although it was unhandy, because it was an island and the only way to get there was by ferry. Or you went by boat for whatever you were doing, so you were much better being out in town.

Q: Was it customary for many Navy junior officers to have their families in Hawaii then?

Capt. O.: Well, all of those who were married. This was counted as sea duty, but we were shore based and this was our home port, so to speak, so the families were there.

Q: This would have been more though for just the Hawaiian detachment than when the fleet came in 1940. They didn't bring their families out, did they?

Capt. O.: Oh, no. That's mentioned in your book that that was one of the things. No, this was a wonderful time in Hawaii. Tom described it quite aptly as being the "seven good years" period that we were going through, but he was positive that the "seven lean ones" were coming and was very prophetic that it really got to be the lean ones. Whether it's exactly seven years or not may be the question. And as he had pointed out also in your book, just immediately before the war started, he had been out to Wake and Midway. So I didn't see too much of him and as a matter of fact, my wife and Carrie were evacuated on the same ship and came back together in mid-January of 1942. I put them on the ship, but I don't remember Tom being there, and I guess that he had already departed on the mission to the East Indies. I did get a note from him sometime up there--which I haven't been able to find--in which he describes the landing that I told you about earlier. We ran into him on several occasions later. We went to the Naval War College in the same class together and he was in Washington when my son was applying to the Academy and I got his endorsement on Bill to go to the Academy. While he was a midshipman, my son visited Hawaii twice on summer vacation and during the time when Tom was CINCPACFLT, Bill used to date his daughter out there. So we have been very close. We visited with him while he was down in Norfolk. We visited Tom and Carrie's parents in Eufala, Alabama, so we have been close personally over all these years. I don't see much of him these days; he's too busy with more important things.

Q: I hear he is very busy.

Capt. O.: To get back to Patrol Wing 2, when I reported, the Commander of Patrol Wing 2 was J. J. Clark, or at least his name appears on my orders. The next name which appears is A. L. Bristol, who frankly I don't remember that well. I was surprised to find Aubrey Fitch as the next one. Then Pat Bellinger. My original recollection without reviewing my orders was I thought he was the first one we had. And finally, Marc Mitscher shows up around the period right after the 7th of December. Interestingly enough, my original orders to report out here told me to report to commanding officer of VP-10. The modifications to that order, which I did not receive until we got there, said to report to VP-25, there having been a change in the number of the squadron. Sometime later in 1940, I believe (although I have no record of the change), the squadron became designated as VP-23. Our first skipper was A. R. "Diamond Jim" Brady out of '22 and our exec was Clarence O. Taff out of '26. Somewhere down the line--and again I'm not sure, but it's probably in mid-1940--Massie Hughes out of '23 took over as skipper and also at a date I don't remember exactly, Bob Winters out of '27 became the exec. He was later killed and I will touch on that as we come up to the time of it.

On arriving, I was next to junior officer--that is before the AvCads, the aviation cadets, were commissioned. I believe that by December of 1941 that all of the original officers and the cadets had left the squadron. I believe of those that came out on the ship with us, that Tom Moorer and I were probably the only officers that I can remember that had been there that long. When the Hawaiian detachment, which is what they called the fleet that moved out there in 1940, when the emergency which caused this thing to happen, all of our orders were frozen. Normally we would have only stayed there two years which was coming up at about that stage of the game. The freeze kept us there until December the 7th, which froze it again for the next year as far as that was concerned.

Q: What had you been expecting? To go into some other type of plane like a fighter?

Capt. O.: Presumably that would have been the normal course of events after we were out there two years, to be detached and of course I say when I reported, people had been there for some while, and they were gradually detached. In those days it seemed that the new people that we got in were all coming from the aviation cadet program and not too many new senior officers were coming in, Bob Winters being one and of course Massie Hughes*. The cadets were commissioned some time during the early 1940s. They were either commissioned or released from duty, so all of our original cadets, I'm sure, went out and new ones came back in and replacements were from later groups. They mostly started showing up as ensigns, and then I'd see them as JGs and finally even some of the earliest of the second group that we had gotten were lieutenants before I left. Immediately after the war began, all of the enlisted pilots were commissioned and they were the backbone in experience of the squadron during the time that we went through with the Midway and Guadalcanal operations and so forth. Like I say, at Midway, two of them were very definitely the ones I would pick to have the experience.

---

*Lieutenant Commander Francis Massie Hughes, USN, commanding officer, VP-23.

Q: They were commissioned right after the war started?

Capt. O.: Yes, I think most of them as JGs and I know one, our chief of the squadron, our leading chief, we certainly recommended him for lieutenant because he was a real type.

Our basing arrangements in Hawaii, prewar, was our permanent base on Ford Island. When we got there, I'm not exactly sure, but I think there were three squadrons, each one with a hangar at the southern tip of Ford Island. When we operated in the early part of the period between the middle of 1939 and when we got there on December the 7th of 1941, when we made trips to Midway and Wake and later at Canton, we used Pan American facilities. They could handle us quite readily with the same facilities they used for the Clippers, particularly in terms of gassing and whatnot, so we didn't need tenders when we went there. Later, it was the same thing at Canton. We had two of the Lapwing-class tenders, the Swan and the Avocet, I think, that we could use at places like Johnston Island and one time at French Frigate Shoals, a couple of times at French Frigate, I guess. Then later, as we started getting a little more money for things, the Navy directed the development of facilities at Palmyra, Johnston, Midway, Wake and of course Kaneohe. During this time we got additional squadrons. Then later when Kaneohe opened, I think we dropped back to three squadrons at Pearl, and they had three. Then some squadrons came through going out to the Philippines.

Our prewar experiences out there--one thing was a very peculiar working arrangement. We worked hours of 7 a.m. to 1 p.m. They said 7 to 1; of course they managed to schedule takeoffs at 6:30 and sometimes 1 o'clock meant 1 o'clock the next morning and not that afternoon. But this was a beautiful working arrangement which incidentally every one of the patrol wing commanders that I've mentioned when he first got there, he put us back on regular 8:00 to 4:00 hours. It took him about a month to find out that that didn't work, so we would go back to 7 to 1. But with the nature of our flights being five or six hours, if not more, these hours worked fine because our maintenance crews, for instance, did not have to stop and put away all their tools and take time out to go somewhere and get lunch, which really wasn't very handy to begin with and then start working over again. So we got six--plus straight working hours out of those crews, and the plane crews could fly and get in full time and not have to worry about anything else again. So it really was more efficient than what would seem like more stable hours, plus the fact that it enabled us to have time to enjoy the things that we did have to do there, to get to the beach. It was interesting to be there in that time frame because we were enabled to see our outlying islands while they were virtually in their pristine state, so to speak. They didn't exactly represent the popular idea of a tropical island, but in some cases it was pretty close, particularly down in Palmyra where I managed to spend a week, having gone down on the Oglala to arrange for some fueling from drums on the beach in case the plane had to go down there, which it might have to do sometime, and a tender wasn't available. For instance, as an example of how the PBY operated, the dredge at Palmyra broke a main crankshaft and we procured one and managed to lash it on to the torpedo rack on the PBY and flew it down there and it saved all kinds of time for the ship in getting this thing going. Also we went down there one time as a hearse. Somebody had died down there, and they needed to return the remains.

I had the good fortune on one of my bombing runs some time in January, probably in 1940 to see the main crater of Mauna Loa in eruption. I'm sure I scared the dickens out of my plane crew, but we were practically down in the crater itself with the middle part of it looking like a pot of Campbell's tomato soup at full boil, with fountains of lava coming up 400 feet or so and one orange stream going down the side of the mountain and a waterfall. It was really quite an impressive sight.

Sometime in 1940, for about six months, I was appointed as extra duty to set up a group of myself and four or five aviation cadets in a little exercise in aerial reconnaissance of beaches in which we were trying to determine with color photographs of the various beaches around there where we could compare known water depths and whether there would be any way in which by taking aerial photographs, we could figure out what the beach characteristics were. It was hard to go in and wading around to find out.

Q: This would be for possible amphibious assault intelligence?

Capt. O.: Yes, that kind of thing. Unfortunately, this was strictly an amateur operation, and I'm afraid not very much came of it. During this time, I made lieutenant and there was a steady stream of different jobs that I had, gradually moving a little up the line. At some time, again I'm assuming the middle of 1940, we have a very definite gas shortage, (I assume more of money than the gas itself.) I noticed by looking in my log books that during this time, our average flight hours per month were 25 to 30. By mid-1941, however, this had increased to 45 to 70 hours a month. This is an indication of the pace of operation during that time.

Q: What kind of flights were you flying mainly during this period?

Capt. O.: It is very hard for me to identify these from my log book because they would probably say "Patrol," which may mean almost anything. But some of the things we were doing apparently didn't fit the categories in which they were marked, or whoever worked on the thing. Obviously we were training because we had new pilots. We had to do the familiarization flying and basic training for pilots, primarily. Flight crews were relatively stable throughout this period. But any time over a period of a couple of years you completely turn over your officer personnel, there is a training problem, very definitely, involved. Our new cadets were coming to us directly out of Pensacola, so they were starting from scratch in an operating unit.

Q: Did you still have the bombing and torpedo work and so forth as you had in Patrol Wing 1?

Capt. O.: We had it, although it was much more on an individual basis than it was as a squadron operation. The torpedo was absolutely negative; we were never exposed to torpedoes out there. As far as I know, and I may be incorrect, somewhere else they had done torpedo work, but I know that as far as my squadron in Hawaii was concerned, there was nobody else there who had probably even seen a torpedo, much less dropped one. I bring this torpedo work up, because it does come up a little bit later. Also, to point out something, during this time but I can't exactly identify the date, there was some new kind of intelligence or a rumor that a mother sub had deposited some half a dozen midget subs and had sunk them in the shallows around the islands for future use. So we combed these beaches and shallows all around the islands very extensively looking for this. I bring this up merely to indicate that when we got intelligence information, even of a minor nature such as this, we really went all out and flew like the dickens looking for it, just like we did back in San Diego when one time, as far as we knew, naval intelligence lost sight of a squadron of motor torpedo boats. We flew like crazy, and I mean like crazy, because we were flying in such bad weather that we lost at least one plane and crew in operational accidents that we would never have been flying under normal circumstances. As I say, this is looking for a squadron of motor torpedo boats. I bring this up really because if we had had any indication that the whole damn Japanese fleet was out somewhere, you can bet your boots we would have been flying more than when we were at this stage of the game.

Q: Were these U.S. torpedo boats off San Diego?

Capt. O.: No, they were Japanese motor torpedo boats. Our intelligence had lost track of them. They didn't know where they were.

Q: Had they been operating off of California?

Capt. O.: We didn't know where they were. You were asking about whether we did any search missions, and there was not much of a search mission back in San Diego, but this was one case where there was some search back there, but obviously nothing came of it. I would assume that most of the search was involved in going down on the Mexican coast to spot. Much has been made of the searches that some people say we should have been making for the protection of the Hawaiian detachment, which is the name that applied to the fleet that came out there under emergency conditions. It existed in the middle of 1941. We were well aware that war was imminent, I think, but we thought it somewhat unlikely that it would affect us directly there.

Q: Why did you think it unlikely? The purpose of sending the fleet out there was because supposedly Japan was hostile.

Capt. O.: Well, the idea that the fleet was there was that it was that much closer to Japan than the West Coast of the United States was, and I think a part of the philosophy of the Navy and its top commanders at that time, obviously (through my own conjecture), is that it was dominated by so-called battleship admirals who expected the war that was coming up to be involved with a crossing-the-"T" battleship fight, which enters into the idea of what are you looking for with these searches, which is what I'm building up to.

Ogden #1 -36

Q: I'm interested in your perception. Was it your belief then that if there was going to be a war it would be somewhere else, that you would go to it rather than it coming to you?

Capt. O.: Right.

Q: Or was there feeling that your were deterring war by being in the forward position?

Capt. O.: My reaction was this: it was funny, having made mention of the fact that we had done so much to find so little in terms of these motor torpedo boats or the midget subs or whatnot, that certainly if we had intelligence information that the Japanese fleet was somewhere other than in Japan, certainly whatever sources of information that we had (and we had just as much, if you will, in the later part of November), in Japan, we had the same intelligen capabilities then that we did back in 1939. If the whole Japanese fleet or a substantial part thereof, including the four carriers that they had, weren't there that somebody would have said, "whoops, and we would have been alerted. In other words, our previous experience with intelligence, to me, indicated that if anything that could bother us at Pearl Harbor was happening, we would have dog-gone well have been on a much, much higher state of alert than we were.

Q: You would have had plenty of warning?

Capt. O.: We would have had plenty of warning to somebody about what we were looking for. I flew back with our squadron to San Diego in November of 1941, the early part of November. We flew back to Hawaii with a new set of airplanes on the 23rd of November.

Q: Was this a newer model?

Capt. O.: Yes, this was the PBY-5. I was amazed to find in San Diego a much greater awareness of the imminence of war. They weren't talking "whether" but "when."

Q: How do you account for that difference?

Capt. O.: I don't know. Obviously we got the same news in the newspaper. It was always a day later or so out there, but again I can only assume that because we had not been alerted, we were not running a patrol that would guard against the kind of attack that we got. I'm getting to the fact that I know we couldn't have maintained any kind of patrol. With what we had, we could not have maintained the patrol--except almost by accident--that would have prevented that attack from taking place as it did.

Q: It sounds as if you almost had a false sense of security, that you had the expectation that you would know about the problem before the newspapers would and you hadn't heard anything like that.

Capt. O.: That's right. That's exactly it.

Q: What were the differences in the models of the PBYs, in the new ones you got?

Capt. O.: Very little. The only difference that was obvious--they did have self-sealing tanks so we had some expectation of...

Q: Of combat?

Capt. O.: Of combat. And they had the blisters that I've described to you instead of the sliding flush doors that gave the plane a Mae West appearance, but otherwise it doesn't change its performance characteristics. We might have had a slightly newer model engine in it, but basically it was the same airplane with the same characteristics.

Q: What happened with the old airplanes that you turned in?

Capt. O.: I wouldn't know, but I assume they ended up back in Pensac for training. Maybe we got them back; I don't know. What happened after the 7th was as makeshift as it's going to be. No, I do think we had supplies, but where they came from I don't know.

The search problem that we had was to protect the fleet at that stage of the game. As I say, to me, the search that would have warned us of this definitely was not a patrol plane search out of Pearl, but a submarine patrol out of Japan that could have done something to keep track of where their fleet was.

Q: You mean a U.S. submarine that would have tracked them?

Capt. O.: Not to track them, but to at least see them come and go or have some idea whether they were in port or when they left or where because here's the problem: if what you are trying to guard against is an aircraft carrier attack, you haven't got anythin like more than a 40% or 50% chance of finding anything by this operation in the first place.

Q: Why not?

Capt. O.: I will have to get ahead of myself to answer that question. When we were out at Midway, we had information exactly where what was going to be. There were two Japanese forces, one of them to the southwest, the other one to the northwest. We knew when they were going to come; we knew that there were going to be carriers in this force and there were going to be landing forces and surface ships in the other force. The day that the main force, including the carriers, was within our 700-mile range, as far as I can tell from this thing, when we should have found them, we didn't find them because they were obscured in the fog. We did find the other force right on schedule, right on the dot. Like I say, we were told they would be bearing $260°$. Don't tell me whose navigation was off on that--whether it was the Japs or ours. But this was the kind of precise information that we had at Midway as opposed to no information in Pearl Harbor as to what we were even looking for or whether it might even be there or not.

To run a search to 700 miles, which you would need to do-- this assumes that you take off at daylight and they're at the far end of the thing around noon and this is a 12-hour hop involved. You go out 700 miles on one bearing covering a $10°$ sector. That puts you 100 miles across the outside section. With the best visibility that you've got, you can't find a fleet outside of about 20 miles. You think a fleet looks pretty damn big, but in perfect visibility and if they're kicking up a wake, you might be able to see them that far. So if you're planning on flying 100 miles across, you've got things spread out like the fingers on a hand at the far end, and you can hide a fleet in each one of those little things out at the far end of the thing. You might find them and you might not. If the weather's bad, you're not going to find anything.

Q: At what altitude would you fly these patrols?

Capt. O.: We would generally fly them at relatively low altitudes, 1,000 to 2,000 feet at the most. This would give you enough; the higher up you got, it didn't help your visibility. The more you were looking down, the less likely you were to see things. If you were looking out, you might see them at greater distances because you could see the mast sticking up against the sky, plus the fact that it improved our navigation capabilities by staying at the lower altitudes because our winds at 1,000 feet and around in that area were not too different from the surface winds and you could always pick up the surface winds visually, by watching the things and you could make corrections in your course so that your searches were right without having to have people not looking while they're going through some navigational procedures, dropping smoke floats to find out what the wind actually was.

Q: Plus, the higher you are, the smaller the ships look.

Capt. O.: Yes, plus the angle at which you look on. The ship gets to be looking awful small. A single ship you're going to have trouble finding at 10 or 15 miles out, regardless of what altitude you're flying, unless he's kicking up one hell of a wake and the water is calm. If you've got some real waves running, you're going to practically get down on top of him. You're running a kind of patrol that isn't very productive. To do this and to cover 220°, which you would probably want to do--there's not much point in trying to cover back towards stateside from out there--so this as opposed to Tom's remark* in there that you'd need 30 some-odd airplanes, I'd say you'd need about 25 airplanes a day. This is flying 12 hours a day. That starts to add up in time and if you're doing it in peacetime and you don't feel that there's much reason to do it and they're beating you around the head and shoulders, the crew's getting tired, they're getting lax, this becomes an all-out effort. I know about this, because down in the South Pacific we were running an all-out effort and we were in a wartime situation and we knew the necessity of doing it. We knew it was something that had to be done, and so we ended up with crews down there flying 250 hours a month, plus or minus, which was more than the whole dog-gone squadron could do at certain stages of this game right in this general time frame because of the gas shortages. So psychologically it was ineffective. Actually it was ineffective and additionally it was so dog-gone expensive, we could never have supported it. It's doubtful whether we could have had enough tankers to bring us the gas to do it. I know that we would have had problems with replacement of engines and in any case, by the time the 7th of December rolled around, that whole dog-gone patrol wing crew would have been in not only a poor state of training, but in a state of utter fatigue, and the planes would be beat up almost as bad as they were after the Japs left there that day.

---

*Admiral Moorer's opinion expressed in <u>Air Raid: Pearl Harbor!</u>, page 20

Q: Well, these were the arguments that the aviators on Admiral Richardson's staff...

Capt. O.: Tried to get Richardson to believe.

Q: Admiral Dyer mentions that Patrol Wing 2 would send up a letter periodically recommending that these flights be called off, as they eventually were, and reduced in scope.*

Capt. O.: Yes.

Q: Also, I think you have a boredom factor of doing the same thing every day. How effective could the lookout be?

Capt. O.: That's exactly the point that we're talking about. When they know, as they did down in the South Pacific, that there's very apt to be somebody out there and that they'd better damn well find out about it as soon as they can, they can be very alert.

Q: And your mind-set also that in these prewar patrols, you figured you would be warned if there was anything to look for.

Capt. O.: Yes. This is involved in specifically an air situation. Now, Dyer mentions a 300-mile patrol. Well, when I read that I didn't quite understand what he was talking about. The only reason to make a 300-mile patrol would be if all you were looking for were battleships and you found them at 300 miles, it would give you time to get your battleships out of the harbor and ready to meet them--if it didn't happen to be on a Sunday morning, when you didn't have them manned all the way anyway. Actually, I

---

*Vice Admiral George Dyer's article in Air Raid: Pearl Harbor!, pages 43-48.

found out yesterday in talking to my classmate Bill Dawson that that 300-mile search that they were talking about was primarily antisubmarine patrol in which the cruiser planes were covering the inboard area and the PBYs were running antisubmarine patrol in the outer. I didn't realize it and didn't remember this in reference to an answer I gave you as to what type of flight it was. My log book doesn't tell me what we were looking for. It just says we were out there looking. I didn't remember that that had been a part of that thing until Bill reminded me, and I did remember that that was what we were doing. So the 300-mile thing turned out to be a submarine search. It would have been effective only against surface ships because if a carrier's within 300 miles of the thing, you aren't going to find the carrier before you get shot down with the planes coming in.

Q: That could have at least provided some warning back to the base, though, to get hold of some fighters.

Capt. O.: Oh, all right, yes. It could have.

Q: The fighter cover over Pearl would have helped, I think.

Capt. O.: Yes, again it would have helped if we had had all of the fighters in Hawaii on alert at 6:30 in the morning every day of the week from the 1st of June, 1941 until the 7th of December, in which case the fighter pilots would have been in the same problem exactly that I just finished saying the PBYs would have been in there. Because you cannot for psychological reasons, personnel reasons in terms of fatigue and everything else and material and financial reasons have kept people operating over an extensive period of time in a wartime situation. I've heard it said that the British always admitted that if the British Navy was ever going to fight the U.S. Navy in war, what they would do is put to sea and steam around and around in circles while the U.S. Fleet stayed in Condition II until they were groggy as all hell, and then they would fight them and that would be the way to beat them. This would have been exactly the sitaution that existed as far as the planes are concerned. If we had to live with any kind of expectation of finding a force of--how many carriers did they have there? Six?

Q: Yes.

Capt. O.: Four involved in the thing and the other two protecting the rest of them out there, as I remember it, which gives me the shivers when I think about it going out there flying that day.

Q: How many PBYs were there at Pearl Harbor during the months just before the Japanese came?

Capt. O.: To the best of my knowledge, your book definitely says there were 36 at Kaneohe, right?

Q: Right.

Capt. O.: Of which they lost the services of 33 that morning, and the only ones that were available were the three that were out flying. As I remember it, we only had three at Pearl at that stage of the game.

Q: Three squadrons?

Capt. O.: Three squadrons. So there were 72* airplanes as of that date. Now, in the period before, that was fluctuating and in addition to everything else, the squadron numbers had changed and I have really lost track of it. I don't remember just when Kaneohe got into operation. To the best of my knowledge, at Pearl we had gotten in somewhere down the line a fourth squadron. As long as we were operating out of Ford Island only, I don't believe we ever had more than four squadrons there, which is 48 planes. When Kaneohe opened up, my guess is that probably they sent two squadrons over there and had two at Pearl and we finally got another one and they finally got another one. But remember that the ones that we had out there to start with, the three that we had out there to start with, and probably the fourth one, were in a pretty good state of training. Also remember that the ones that were coming out to augment the thing had a few experienced people but not many. I say we were able because the way we were doing out there and the long period of time that we had, we were able to train our aviation cadets and newly commissioned officers. They provided the bulk of the squadrons' pilots. I've said we had several APs

---

*See "Why Were We Caught Napping At Pearl Harbor?" Saturday Evening Post, May 24, 1947, Page 76, by Seth W. Richardson (General Counsel for the Joint Congressional Investigating Committee). He gives the figure 60 as number of PBYs at Pearl Harbor but without a specific date or period. This article also notes the impracticality of conducting "even a partial long-distance patrol" over a long period of time with the forces available. The reasons for reaching such a conclusion are quite similar to mine expressed in several places throughout this interview. I was not aware of the existence of this article when the interview was conducted.

in our squadron, but I don't believe the new squadrons had that source and they were relying on very few--four or five--experienced pilots and the rest of them were aviation cadets or newly commissioned former aviation cadets.

Q: Was there any difference in skills as pilots between the people who came in as aviation cadets as opposed to...

Capt. O.: Oh, no, no. I'm not saying that at all. As a matter of fact, excuse me, I ended up with the squadron and my exec (although I don't know that he was ever designated as such; he just happened to be the next senior guy--Howard Ady out of the Class of '39. I guess he went to Pensacola right off, so he got out of Pensacola in mid-1940.) By the time of Midway, he was one of the three people that I had in the sector where we were going to find the main force carriers and battleships. At that same stage of the game ex-cadets Joe Kellam and Norm Brady (whom you'll hear about later) were as good pilots as you would find anywhere. I'm speaking only in terms of their experience in PBYs because right out of Pensacola, that does take a little bit of doing to have them qualify. These people had served their apprenticeship as second pilots and third pilots for lots of years out there.

Q: So how did the events go then after you brought the next planes back out, just before the start of the war?

Capt. O.: Let me make one more comment on this patrol arrangement before that to set the stage for what goes on. Apparently, at some stage of the game, even this 300-mile antisubmarine patrol jointly with the cruiser planes was abandoned and that was what Dyer was talking about as much as anything else. He mentioned the 300-mile thing, and I don't know what connotation that had at the time, but I do now. The final result and what was in effect at the time of Pearl Harbor December the 7th was an antisubmarine patrol of the fleet operating areas in use. They had numbered areas around Pearl Harbor where battleships or cruisers or destroyers or whatever would go to operate and train. So what we were doing, because the daily requirements would obviously vary, the arrangement was that Pearl Harbor and Kaneohe would alternate, one having six duty planes and the other outfit would have six standby planes so that on any given day if they needed seven airplanes to patrol the operating areas, they would take all six of the duty planes and the standby would provide one. If they didn't use all of them, as Kaneohe didn't on the morning of the 7th (they only used three), they had three sitting on the ground and my six over in Pearl were sitting on the ground. I was there with the group that morning for that purpose. So that was the kind of arrangement that we had. Can we go back to your question?

Q: I think you've covered it right there - the final disposition leading up to the attack.

Capt. O.: That was the arrangement that we had as far as planes. I thought you were asking about the assignment of planes and squadrons.

So then we get to the situation of the 7th of December. I

had a beautiful view, as it turned out, the third deck of corner room of BOQ [bachelor officers' quarters], which was at the northwest corner of Ford Island while our planes were at the complete southern tip as I showed you. Parked a hundred yards or so away was the Utah off of my starboard bow as I looked down the length of the island, down the runway to where our hangars were. We were not awakened at 6:30 and were not warned that our services would be used that day. We normally went off that duty at 8:00 o'clock. I had gotten up at a quarter to 8:00 and was in the shower. Ford Island was a rather funny thing on acoustics and seismology or whatever you call it, but on that place the coral formations of the island were such that every time a cane train came along Aiea, you could feel the vibrations all over the place. It was sort of a floating island almost. Obviously, in the shower I didn't hear very much, but when I got out of the shower, airplanes were flying around, and I thought the stupid dog-gone Army aviators didn't know enough to stay in bed on Sunday morning. There were some rather loud noises and vibration on the island going on and I went to the window with a towel around me. A bunch of black smoke was coming up from down there near our hangars. They did have a trash dump down there, and I said it was very, very peculiar that they would be burning trash on Sunday morning. I couldn't figure that one out and I looked over towards Barbers Point and Ewa, and here was a TBD* steaming up, and I said, "Good God, that guy's going against the course rules," because we were all supposed to steer

---

*TBD was the designation for a U.S. Navy torpedo plane then in the fleet.

Ogden #1 -49

out and go down that way, but we didn't come back that way. It kept on coming and got up approaching Pearl City over where the Pan Am docks were, and the plane had a torpedo on it. I thought that was really peculiar. Then he turned and headed right for me. Then he dropped the torpedo and of course I was in a three-ring circus watching that torpedo track coming across and about the same time this guy ducked up over the Utah and banked by my window about 50 feet away. I could practically see the configuration of his eyes. The thing that struck me particularly was the great big round meatballs around each of one of those wings. Let's say I was surprised.

Q: You decided it wasn't a TBD after all.

Capt. O.: I decided it wasn't a TBD, and I noticed that the Utah had just received its calling card, and so I knew it was for real. I say it's a little bit confused as to what happened then. I do know that I was caught with my pants off which I rapidly corrected, but that's about all. I went below and there were women and children from the quarters, the few that were there, piling into the basement of this BOQ, which is a concrete building. At some time, some kind soul must have come by and offered us transportation, because I got down to the ramp at I would guess 8:20 or so.

Q: And you were in the BOQ that night because you had that duty?

Capt. O.: Yes, because I had that duty. As I pointed out to you, we were not exactly expecting that kind of thing to happen on a Sunday morning. But we got down to the squadron area. Tom Moorer's squadron, in spite of his comment that most of this stuff happened by strafing, I do know that the squadron hangar was hit with bombs, and I think they were 250-pounders that they got. His planes were either in the hangar or very tightly packed, and they had a very small ramp on the far side of the hangar. So they had maybe eight or nine planes or something like that, maybe ten. Later, as far as I know, much later somebody just came in and took a bulldozer and pushed what was left off to one side. Then along the front of the hangar, I'm sure that some of our planes were parked, and those were the ones that when I got back the next day, you could see the outline of the PBY in ashes on the ground. The other hangar that was in use right opposite of his--there were three of them--this one had gotten two bombs, I think, through the roof which didn't set off any fires, but they destroyed the planes that were in the hangar. Our hangar didn't get anything, so when I got there, a plane was rolled out. It was gassed up and it was ready to go. Whether it had been parked outside and managed to escape or whether it was in the hangar and the crews had rolled it out by the time I got there, this I don't know.

Q: Was it your normal plane?

Capt. O.: Don't ask me. I can look it up. I can find the number, but at that stage of the game, we really didn't have a normal plane because we had been doing everything as individuals and you just took whichever plane was basically available. I'm sure that I had one assigned, but I didn't necessarily fly with it at all times.

Q: I got the impression from Admiral Moorer's article that he went first because it was his plane that was ready.

Capt. O.: He was talking about his flight on Monday apparently not realizing I had flown a search the day before.

Well, like I say, we had to provide six planes. At that stage of the game, I know I was not the exec. We had six planes in a division and the skipper had one of them and the exec had the other one. But as a sort of command duty officer, I had six planes and whichever of the six planes were ready to fly that morning, if I had been called that morning to go out, I would have probably have picked my plane to fly if it was one of the six on stand-by. But otherwise, you just take whichever one that's sitting there and what's first in line because its enlisted crew would be in it, but the pilots could be anybody.

Q: I see.

Capt. O.: When I got to the squadron hangar there was obviously much confusion. However, the ground and plane crews who had made everything ready for an earlier flight, if one had been needed, were still there. Most of our planes which were out in the open were damaged or destroyed. There was one plane, which I assume had been in our undamaged hangar, that was being prepared for flight. Shortly after I arrived, our skipper Massie Hughes showed up. His quarters were on Ford Island, so he had wheels. With pants over his pajamas, he had dashed to wing headquarters for instruction. There he had been given a search sector from the plan drawn up by Logan Ramsey that morning after an earlier report of a submarine sighting.* I assume that Ramsey thought this assignment would be the first of several, rather than the only one to be actually conducted, but it was probably the most likely sector in which to find something. In any case, Massie saw me and the plane ready to go and said, "Come on, Jimmy, I've got this search sector so we'll got out and look for them. Pick yourself a crew." I guess the regular plane crew was with the plane, but I was looking for another pilot and some people to man the guns who could hit something. Fortunately, I was the Gunnery Officer at the time so didn't have too much trouble picking "Swede" Thueson** for the third pilot and bow gun position and a couple of sharpshooters for the waist gun positions. But anyway, with a makeshift crew, we took off without many of the formalities. Massie and I were in the pilot seats and normally the skipper would have been at the controls, but for some reason protocol was bypassed and I made the takeoff and landing and most, if not all, of the flying that day.

We stood not on the order of our going. As soon as the beaching gear was off, there was no thought of wind direction, channel or warmup--the throttles went on full and we headed generally toward Middle Loch. During the takeoff I did notice some heavy timbers that caused me to do some juggling to avoid hitting them with my wing-tip floats. I have always thought they came from the topsides

---

*Lieutenant Commander Logan C. Ramsey, USN, operations officer, Patrol Wing 2. See Air Raid: Pearl Harbor!, page 35.
**Theodore S. Thueson, then an enlisted pilot, later commissioned Ensign, USN.

of the remote control target ship Utah when she overturned. In any case, I made a mental note this would be something to bear in mind on our return--when, as, and if.

Q: You did this takeoff right in the channel, sort of in the northwest side of the island?

Capt. O.: It was not our regular channel. It was just water and I could see far enough ahead that I knew I could get off before I got there. So this was strictly an unorthodox takeoff but the best I could do at the moment.

Q: How much water did you normally need for the takeoff run?

Capt. O.: I never thought about it in terms of whether it was a five iron or a pitching wedge, but this was a pitching wedge takeoff run. There wasn't any driver.

Q: You knew by eye what you needed?

Capt. O.: Yes. I really wasn't looking for altitude because as soon as we got airborne and my wingtips were up, I took off for Barbers Point at such a level that if the tail gunner wanted to, he could have cut cane all the way. Fortunately, I found out later, (I'm really not sure about it) that one of my gunners had expended all of his ammunition before we got to Ewa. But I didn't think we had been attacked at the time. I didn't know whether to believe it or not.

Q: He expended it before what happened?

Capt. O.: Before we got to Barbers Point, he had shot up all of his ammunition on the way out with somebody coming after us, but I find it unlikely that anybody could have missed me. But later we did have one, not under those exact circumstances, we did have an occasion down in the South Pacific where a PBY ran six Jap fighters out of ammunition and got away. That takes some flying, I promise you. But I was just getting out at this stage of the game.

Q: The attack was still in progress when you took off?

Capt. O.: There seemed to be a lull. I did not see any fighters making strafing runs. I assumed the fighters, at this stage of the game, were otherwise occupied and we were on the opposite side of Ford Island from any torpedo planes or dive-bombers that were making runs. They wouldn't have bothered with me anyway, because they had something else to shoot at. I would assume that my only problem on takeoff would have been fighters. The rest of the people were busy with what they came to do and they weren't looking for planes, I guess.

Q: You've told me that you took off about 8:30. Would it be fair to say to you were the first U.S. Navy plane to get off during the attack?

Capt. O.: No, no, not U.S. Navy plane. There were carrier planes there. I'm sure the Enterprise didn't have all of her airplanes aboard. There were people that were taking off in anything that was available. They had some amphibious biplanes, J2F is what they call them. People were getting up in anything that they could throw a rock out of, as far as I know. I would by no means assume that I was the first one up. But I was the first—as far as I know—the only one to get off in a PBY.

Q: I see. And so what was your sector then?

Capt. O.: I have tried to reconstruct that as best I can and only from the memory, the vague memory. We had gone by the southern side of Kauai on the way out and we'd come back around the northern edge of Kauai on the way back. I don't have the actual charts available and I don't know exactly whether the sector origin was Barbers Point or whether it was Ford Island or Makapuu Point or wherever. But this would put it in the range of going out about $285°$ and coming back in on a $10°$ or so difference, the reverse of $300°$ whatever that is. One hundred twenty, right, coming back in. So the outgoing sector between roughly $285°$ or $290°$ and $300°$ in that range coming back in.

I found something and fortunately it didn't turn out to be fatal, although I'm sure it startled everybody in both sides of it; we passed the <u>Enterprise</u> and the cruiser division that was with it. Fortunately my years in the cruisers, two before Pensacola and two after it, I was thoroughly familiar with the outline of the cruisers. They were the first things I saw and so we didn't panic, although we were rather close aboard because of the haze we had at that time. It was too late to change courses and surprisingly enough, I seem to remember that I kept thinking of recognition signs and I guess being aviators, they recognized a PBY when they saw it and I don't think the Japs had anything that looked exactly like it. We didn't have any established recognition signals that we could have flashed by light. We had flashing lights that we could use to signal with, but we did not exchange recognition signals like "good morning" or anything else and they went on their way. I do not remember if they were receiving planes on deck. I know that they were coming back in to Pearl and from the distance out, which I don't remember exactly--roughly 100 miles or something in that order--that they had sent their planes ahead. It would have been normal procedure, I think, for them to send their planes in ahead of time. I do know the planes came in and I do know they did end up in dog fights that morning. Of course there was a series in the Saturday Evening Post a long time ago about Dickinson's "I fly for vengeance" type of thing and he was apparently shot down three times that day, which didn't speak very much of anything, but that's the kind of stuff that was going on.*

Q: What kind of planes did you see from the Enterprise? Were these fighters?

Capt. O.: I say no, I didn't see any airplanes airborne. I don't know whether the Enterprise had already launched its planes. I didn't notice any on deck.

Q: So it was the ships themselves that you sort of said "good morning" to, not their planes?

---

*See Clarence Dickinson, Saturday Evening Post, 17 October 1942, page 22. Also Dickinson, The Flying Guns: Cockpit Record of a Naval Pilot from Pearl Harbor Through Midway (New York: Scribner's, 1942).

Capt. O.: No, no, we did not see any of their planes airborne. By merely saying that I hadn't noticed any planes, we had passed very close aboard it and we were not very high at that stage of the game and with the haze, we were within five miles of the Enterprise. I mean, by the time I saw the ships, we were there. They were not in a launch characteristic, because the cruisers were definitely in readiness position all around it.

The rest of that flight was a weird one. I won't say it was thrilling, but it was cause for thought. First, one of the impressions I had--Massie sitting, I believe, in the left seat and the incongruity of seeing his pajama legs sticking out from under his pants. The thing I remember most is that his running remarks throughout, of rather an obscene nature, were applied more to U.S. Congressmen than they were to Japanese, in view of the flak we had been getting. Which was another reason for my firm conviction later that FDR had withheld information on purpose and that the purpose was served by having it happen the way it did, rather than our making a move first, or anything that could have been construed as a move or we might have had another Vietnam reaction in Congress. But by the by, the rest of it was wondering what the hell was happening back home on both Ford Island and out in town. The out in town part involved one of the old stories that used to go around out there. Practically all of us had Japanese maids or Japanese-American maids and with the dual citizenship, you never did really know which took precedence, even for the ones that did have U.S. citizenship. But the story used to be that someone decided to ask their maid, "If we have a war with Japan, do you kill us?"

She said, "Oh, no, you my master. I kill Mr. Jones, and Mr. Jones' maid kill you." Well, you didn't really believe that, but damn it, when you're sitting out there and you have a Japanese maid at home, a young bride and a young year-old child, you start to wondering what's going on back there. Then you sit there and you say, "I wonder who's in charge back at Ford Island." Nobody tells you anything and you go on and then you start wondering, "Suppose we find this group. What then?" And in addition to thinki "I guess we'll be able to get off the plain-language dispatch before we get shot down, but if we do, is anybody going to hear it? And if they hear it, what in the hell can they do about it?" Because I knew that the Enterprise was not in any position--I didn't think she was in a position to launch even if we found out where it was and make sure they weren't going to send off any planes until they found out where they were going to go, by that time they would be to hell and gone and so what? I mean, it gives you cause to think, "Why am I doing this in the first place? Suppose I do what I'm supposed to do?" But we didn't close our eyes. It might have been a historical thing but it could have been a personal catastroph

Q: Did you hear anything on the radio during this patrol?

Capt. O.: Not word number one. All right, so we came back around 8:30 in the evening after a 12-hour hop or somewhere in that neighborhood. It was definitely after dark. It was black as the inside of a cow. When we got to Barbers Point, in the first place it was raining like hell and in the second place, we tried to call somebody on the radio and got no answer. I don't know whether it was because we weren't transmitting or because nobody was listening at the other end. From some of the accounts in the book, I decided that whether or not my radio was out, there wasn't anybody listening to our voice transmissions. We didn't have any recognition signals anyway, so the first thing to do was to try to act as friendly as possible, and that meant turning on every light that we could think of because only a damn fool would try to come in in the dark. So the next idea was where to land. Under normal circumstances, the landing area closest to our ramp would have been the Dry Dock Channel, but the Dry Dock Channel had dredging rigs there and long, big pipes to take the spoil somewhere, so that narrowed the channel down in the dark, and the only light on the island anyway was the _Arizona_ burning, which wasn't much help in making a night landing. So hopefully, we decided that the best bet would be the Pearl City channel and hope that somebody had the foresight to go out there in the day and clear up the debris in the channel. Well, this was a very fortunate decision because had we elected to come in the other channel (which incidentally had a row of approach lights right on the edge of the land as you were making your approach) the next morning the _Nevada_ was firmly beached right smack-dab alongside those landing lights, and if we had come in and hadn't seen them in time, we'd have landed right in the mast of the _Nevada_. But we didn't. We landed over in the other place and somebody was thoughtful enough to remove the debris and we went cheerfully along our way, acting friendly as all get-out. But at about that stage of the game, four fighter planes from the Enterprise did come in, and they didn't take the precaution of acting friendly, so people got unfriendly on the beach and this started the biggest firework display that has been seen in Hawaii, including all the Chinese New Years put together. We were only seeing one round in five, but the tracers lit up the sky like crazy and the shrapnel and everything was falling around like it was rain in the water. During the day, the guns for 35 airplanes were in the unharmed armories of the three hangars, and they had all been deployed around the parking areas and they had joined in the celebration. The Army was shooting off some of their small antiaircraft stuff. I feel reasonably sure in saying that all four of these planes were shot down, but rumors were going around all over the place about anything, and some of them were true and some of them weren't true. But at least some of them were. But this got to be a hairy operation, because every once in a while I got the impression that they were shooting at us, so I turned off the lights so they didn't have any good aiming point and somebody would see our exhaust flames or hear the noise and then start acting unfriendly, so I turned the lights back on again and finally we got to the ramp and were aboard.

I don't know what happened. I'm sure we went to the headquarters and were briefed that night. I know I spent the night at Massie's house.

Q: Do you know if you got shot at in reality?

Capt. O.: No, I don't remember that our plane had any holes in it, although as it was also reported in your book in Tom's article, that on a space the size of this room on the ramp, you could go out and pick up 20 pieces of shrapnel on it. And yet I don't remember that we were hurt, nobody was hurt in the plane and I don't believe that the plane was damaged. It's almost unbelievable, but unbelievable things happen.

The story was going around which I was able to verify not long ago when I was talking to Joe Cobb who was over in Kaneohe, and the story over there was that they expected an airborne landing.* So during the day, they parked fuel trucks, oil barrels, everything else in a random pattern all over the landing field, but sometime during the night a fighter, F4F, came over there to make a landing without any warning or any instructions from the tower or anything else, proceeded to land and taxi off of the field without hitting anything. They said the next morning they took him down there and showed him what he had landed in and he fainted dead away, which I can readily understand because it was unbelievable that they had done this design so that nobody could make any kind of a landing and here this guy comes in, black as the ace of spades and not hit a thing. It took some of the wind out of their sails in their method of distributing obstacles.

Q: So you went to the skipper's house that night?

---

*Lieutenant James O. Cobb, USN, a PBY pilot at Kaneohe.

Capt. O.: Yes. I seem to remember--and this is something about Tom account that I can't quite understand--I was under the impression that somewhere that night, possibly at headquarters, I had run into Tom Moorer. In Honolulu that day, they just cut off telephone service completely and they wouldn't let you call anything. That night around midnight, my wife said, our phone rang and it was Carrie's voice on the phone, she didn't identify herself but Carrie said, "Tom says to tell you Jimmy's all right." Click. She hung up. She got that much out. So Tom had called her during the day and apparently had seen me and I presume he knew that I had been flying that day. But I guess that he thought, when he made the statement that he made the first flight out the next day, sometime during the middle of the next day, that he had either not known that I was flying that day or had assumed that I had gone out before the attack.

Q: Because he didn't know that something had happened to you?

Capt. O.: Well, he knew that nothing had happened to me enough to tell his wife. I don't think he would have said that just to make somebody feel better and then find out it wasn't true. I think he saw me and knew that I was there and maybe he told me he was going to call. He must not have known of my flight; otherwise, he would not have made the remark that his flight was the first one out.

Q: You'll have to tell him that the next time you see him.

Capt. O.: Well, I certainly intend to. The thing about that particular thing is that at Tom's retirement ceremony - as I said, there were a whole bunch of classmates there all together, and when Dr. Schlesinger was giving his dissertation on Tom's career he made the remark that Tom was in the first PBY to take off from Pearl Harbor after the raid.* And I turned to the people next to me and said, "Tom Moorer has got so damn many things in the world to be proud of and what he's done, why does he have to take away the only dad-gone thing I've got going for me?"

---

* James R. Schlesinger, Secretary of Defense at the time of Admiral Moorer's retirement ceremony in 1974.

Interview No. 2 with Captain James R. Ogden

Place: At his home in Annapolis, Maryland

Date: March 16, 1982

Subject: Captain Ogden's experiences in Naval Aviation

By: Paul Stillwell

Q: Captain, when we left off last week, we had just finished recounting your experiences on December 7, 1941 returning from your patrol that day. Would you like to pick it up from there, please?

Capt. O.: Okay. My log book shows very few flights during the remainder of December. My job primarily was being down at our hangar, which was the only one undamaged of the patrol plane squadrons and briefing the pilots that we had going out on patrol. As I remember, we had very few planes at that stage of the game, and most of those were then brought over to Pearl Harbor, including the three or four that were available from Kaneohe. All patrol planes were originally being run out of Pearl. During this time (this period was until the Friday following before I got home) we all stayed out there. Everybody slept in a hangar and it provided a lot of togetherness.

Q: Could you recount the mood during that time, the sense of apprehension, whatever you felt?

Capt. O.: It was a feeling of shock, obviously. Things were going on more or less in a dream, people were jittery and that brings up some of the things that I can account and can show you how that goes. For instance, during the night on several occasions, we would hear the Marine sentry's challenges which went in rapid order: "Halt, Halt, Halt," Bang! This made travelling around the area after dark something of an adventure. My job of briefing and debriefing of the pilots on these patrols required that after all the planes were in and reports were made, that I would carry the word back to the wing command post which was at the extreme northern end of Ford Island. Since this was a little bit too far to walk, I used to go in a putt-putt, a motor scooter. Well, going along almost every night, I would hear a sentry say, "Halt!" and not knowing which one it was, I immediately bailed out, which was hard on the knees and whatnot, but it managed to work. Also, dealing with sounds in the night--I say we were all living in the hangar, and that meant that for ventilation we would normally have the hangar doors open, but one night apparently it must have been raining because somebody decided to close the hangar doors. Well, anyone who is not familiar with the way a hangar door operates, when it moves, it takes several people to move it and once you get going, it picks up a certain amount of momentum and this happened. When it hit the opposing door, the sound was remarkably like that of a 500-pound bomb just outside, which cleared the hangar in record time, I assure you.

Q: What was your position in the squadron? You've mentioned that you were debriefing. Were you operations or intelligence?

Capt. O.: This is an interesting idea, because up until about this time, my records are replete with duty assignments and somehow or other, along about this stage of the game, that all went out the window, and everything was dependent upon who just happened to be next senior because people were coming and going. As I remember, I had been the gunnery officer at the time, so I assumed that I still was. But why this job devolved on me, I really can't tell.

Q: What was the purpose of the patrols you were sending out at that point?

Capt. O.: We were going out looking to see if there was any follow up, presumably. I say that we were just doing whatever we could and our job was to patrol. Where they told us to patrol I don't know. A part of the thing that we were doing was to report on where our ships were so that there would be no confusion. In this connection, one ship in which I was particularly interested was the William Ward Burrows, which was mentioned [in Air Raid: Pearl Harbor!]. This was a ship which was primarily responsible for the support of the work that was going on at Wake and the outlying islands. According to some reports that I've seen, she had left Johnston and was coming back, but my understanding was that she had been ready to go into Wake. The reason that I was interested is that her executive officer was married to a cousin of my wife's who was out there, and I know that she was quite interested in finding out. I couldn't tell the whereabouts, but

I could tell her it was there somewhere.

Q: And presumably safe.

Capt. O.: And presumably still chugging.

Q: Admiral Moorer, in his oral history, said that his lookouts on his PBY were much more attentive after the war started. Did you find that same phenomenon?

Capt. O.: Well, at this stage of the game, I wasn't doing that much flying, myself. Like I say, there couldn't have been much more starting off than about half a dozen planes and gradually working up. This is with all kinds of pilots around to do things. My memory doesn't come back about these things which were just of routine nature, unless they were really something to really make me remember or things like the few little things that happened on the island in the immediate time after the thing.

For instance, I remember going up to the dispensary since I had heard they had been hit by a bomb. The dispensary was a fairly new building, a hollow square with a fountain and a little thing in the middle. Apparently, one of the Japanese pilots, attempting to bomb the California, which was right next to it, had overshot and his bomb--which was presumably an armor-piercing projectile with a time delay fuse on it--had gone down directly through the middle of this fountain and had gone off down below. Because of the soft coral down there, it had not really wrecked the fountain that much and had broken no windows in the building and had injured no one there with reportedly casualties all flaked out over the whole inner patio in the place.

Another little incident which is sort of funny in its way-- it has been reported in several of the accounts about the midget subs which had gotten into the harbor. I remember one in particular where one of our submarine crew's men had been working on the sonar and had a contact and it presumably was verified to be one of the midget subs. Well, we got a plane in the air with a depth bomb on it, but we didn't think it would be very effective because our depth bombs had a minimum depth of 50 feet before going off. So they decided to try something else and got a motor torpedo boat that was capable of using a depth charge with a 25-foot setting and still be able to get out of the way before it got him. The problem was to accurately locate the midget sub, and this is undoubtedly one of the most unusual submarine location systems ever developed because it consisted of a guy in a 50-foot motor launch with a long pole, going along and poking down into the water until he heard it go "clink" instead of "squish."

Q: How soon after the attack was that?

Capt. O.: Well, it had to have been in the first two or three days.

Q: I see.

Capt. O.: The reason that we had to do something about it, really, was that one of the hospital ships was in the line of fire, so to speak, and it was up in the Aiea section of the harbor. The only other funny thing, I guess you would call it, a personal affair, is as I might have mentioned earlier, the stories that were always going around in Hawaii were about the dual citizenship Japanese and the story that somebody asked his maid, "If we have a war, are you going to kill me?"

And she said, "Oh, no, you my master. Mr. Jones' maid kill you. I kill Mr. Jones." Well, this hadn't made the day of the 7th very comfortable with my wife at home with a Japanese maid. When I did get back on Friday, my maid was more anxious to see me than my wife was, it seemed like, almost, because she had not been at home on the morning of the 7th, but had been downtown and she rushed home. Incidentally, the part of town that she was in was hit by a bomb, so she came closer to damage than Betty did. But when she got back, she started packing immediately and Betty asked her what would she do and she said, "Well, obviously you don't want me to stay here with you." But Betty assured her that we very definitely did want her to. She talked her into staying, but the maid said, "Only if master, when he comes home, says I can stay." So she was there waiting frantically to see whether I would let her stay.

Q: And you did?

Capt. O.: I did. Oh, yes. In the first place, her brother was in the U.S. Army and she was devoted to our daughter.

From there on, from January to May, there was a gradual buildup of the planes.

Q: Where were they coming from? Out from San Diego?

Capt. O.: Yes, they were all coming from San Diego. I still don't quite remember how we got enough pilots back there, or whether they went by surface transportation or air or both, I would assume, at that stage of the game. Of course Pan Am was running the Clipper back and forth and once there was a group--I don't know exactly how many--of PB2Ys which were four-engine versions of the PBY, and quite a bit larger and would carry a lot of people. In this connection, we lost our executive officer on the 6th of May as he was going back in one of the PB2Ys which crashed on takeoff at Pearl.

Q: And his name was what?

Capt. O.: That was Bob Winters.*

Q: How soon after the attack would you say the squadron was back up to full strength?

Capt. O.: I really don't know. I doubt that our squadron was actually up to snuff until May. The squadrons were going and coming during that period of time and the numbers had been changed. Tom Moorer's squadron went off to the Dutch East Indies very definitely sometime earlier than that because I heard from him that practically all of their planes were lost. Two squadrons had gone before the war out to the Philippines and they were pretty much left down in Australia. I do know that the squadrons were brought up to date with new planes and included a number of the

---

*Lieutenant Commander Robert C. Winters, USN.

PBY-5As, which were an amphibious version of the PBY, actually just with the addition of retractable landing gear.

Q: At what point did radar become part of the picture? What difference did that make?

Capt. O.: Our squadron, to the best of my knowledge, was the first to acquire an airborne radar, certainly in the Pacific. This had what they called a Yogi antenna and was strictly side-looking. It was developed, to the best of my knowledge, by the British because the person that briefed us on how to use it and helped with the installation was a British sergeant.

Q: Approximately when was that introduction?

Capt. O.: I really can't remember, but I would say it was probably in the early part of May. In any case, we were the only ones to have it at the time we went out to Midway. I presume that that was one of the reasons we were selected to go.

Q: Does your log show when that deployment to Midway was made?

Capt. O.: This whole period of time I find very difficult to relate. In seeing the accounts of Midway and reading the accounts of Midway and preparations for it from the book on Midway, Walter Lord indicates that by the 15th of May, the intelligence people had decided that the attack was going to be on Midway, but had no specifics.*
It wasn't until perhaps the 25th of May before we got the final

---

*Walter Lord, Incredible Victory (New York: Harper & Row, 1967).

breakdown of the actual forces. In my opinion, I seem to remember having been given a thorough briefing as much as three weeks before the battle which would have put it around the 15th of May.

Q: Do you remember where that briefing came from? Was that from Pacific Fleet Headquarters?

Capt. O.: That briefing was in Patwing 2 headquarters, presumably by Logan Ramsey or possibly by Admiral Bellinger himself.* I don't know. I do know that before going out to Midway, we stopped six of the B-26s that were coming through on their way to the Southwest Pacific and they were told that they were going to become torpedo bombers and that of the six, Captain Collins was the head man.** Because of my previous experience with torpedoes back at Patrol Wing 1, I was selected to go out and check him out on our torpedo dropping procedures. The B-26 was a notoriously erratic airplane in that it caused numerous pilot and crew casualties from various and sundry malfunctions. It was a very fast plane, including its landing procedures. Of these six planes, they busted up two of them rather thoroughly before they left Pearl Harbor just trying to land on Ford Island, which is a short runway for that type of plane. In any case, the aerial torpedoes that we had at that time were not supposed to be able to stand more than a drop at about 72 knots from an altitude of 50 feet. So in attempting to get Collins down to this low speed, for him, and at that altitude, my practice run didn't last very long before

---

*Rear Admiral Patrick N. Bellinger, USN, Commander Patrol Wing 2.
**Captain James F. Collins, Jr., USAAF. See W. F. Craven and J. L. Cate, The Army Air Forces in World War II, Volume I, Plans and Early Operations (Chicago: The University of Chicago Press, 1948), page 458.

his decision that the airplane was going to kill him before the enemy was if he had to do that. So I scratched off, mentally, the B-26 as being much of anything that was going to help our process out there. But the four of them did go and unfortunately, I think only one of them actually was able to fly back from it. Several of them were lost, as history already tells.

In any case, by the time that we did go out to Midway (and again, my log books don't seem to show it), I was sure that we had been out there during the latter part of May but to that I can't be sure. VP-23, with the regular seaplanes were assigned to the ramps and hangars of East Island and VP-44, which had the 5As with the landing gear, were on Sand Island where the only land plane runway on Midway was.

Q: You were in VP-44 then?

Capt. O.: No, I say VP-23 was on the ramp side. We had the seaplanes.

Q: Oh, I thought you said earlier that you had gotten the 5As.

Capt. O.: Oh, no. I said the 5As came out there and my records show as having flown them because planes were there and we more or less had a pool. It really wasn't that much of a squadron operation right after Pearl Harbor. It was a catch-as-catch-can.

Flying out to Midway, because the 5As were heavier than we were to begin with, each plane in our squadron carried out torpedoes. We had 12 torpedoes out there presumably for the six TBFs that they had flown out there or taken out to Midway.* Then also, for the B-26s. We took them out and then they were rowed over to the other island to use over there.

Q: What were the living accommodations for your squadron there?

Capt. O.: There was a hangar there. As far as I remember, we lived in an underground quarters, just bunks. I don't know where the food came from, but we got sandwiches, I guess, or whatever. Everybody was flying almost all day long anyway. Everybody was flying.

Q: So it was more primitive than Hawaii had been?

Capt. O.: Oh, for heaven's sake, it was primitive in more ways than one. When we got there, we found that the defenders, so that they would be able to deny their Japanese anything if they took it over, very carefully rigged all of the gasoline tank farm with explosives and my story as to how it happened is that they very carefully locked up the switches to throw this. As most everything was done out at Midway, one Marine went along with a stick and made a groove in the sand and somebody came along with a line and put sand over it on the way back. Somewhere down the line, they put it right over a telephone line and so when anybody dialed the thing, it blew up the whole gas tank. In any case, the gas tanks were utterly destroyed. Some of

---

*TBFs were U.S. Navy torpedo planes.

them were destroyed and it did destroy all of the distribution lines, so we had no gas in a normal gassing system down at our ramp and therefore had to do all of our fueling from drums. Each plane had a small pump that could be used to gas in this way, but they were not built for doing it as often as we were doing it out there. So these things got to be a little bit scarce a little later.

Q: What about maintenance facilities? Were they also primitive?

Capt. O.: Well, in essence, when we had flown out, we had very little except the actual plane crews we took out, but I presume we did take as many of our squadron maintenance people out as we could get. That was not more than, let's say, about 10 or 15 people. We just flew what we had. Now, at the time of the attack, we had one plane which had broken its back in a rough water landing or a takeoff and so it had been completely cannibalized of virtually everything and we had another one which, when we got down to it, had had so many things taken from it that it wasn't effective as a search plane and we were saving that for a getaway plane, so to speak, in case we had a chance to do it.

Going back a little bit, as I've read over Walter Lord's accounts, the presence of an American seaplane tender at French Frigate Shoals deterred the Japanese from using French Frigate as a base for their seaplanes to come in and scout Pearl Harbor. The reason for that was that it was out there to refuel the motor torpedo boats that were being sent out and then as a place that our planes could go back into the after the attack, if need be. Again, the Lord account seems to indicate some difference in the dates of the attack. As I understand it, my recollection is that when we got out there, we expected the attack to come on the 3rd of June and that therefore we would find to the southwest the landing force at a distance of 600 miles bearing 260° and that we should encounter the striking force to the northwest presumably, if we found them at all, towards the end of our search the day before. On the 2nd of June search, nothing was found in either area where the Japanese were expected to be. The area to the northwest was completely covered with a fog bank. On the 3rd of June, however, the landing force was sighted by VP-44, which had the southern half of our 180° sector that we were searching, bearing 261°, distance 600 miles. This is how good our information was. The striking force was not sighted, again because of weather, although we felt sure that it was there. So we definitely knew then that the aircraft attack on Midway was going on schedule for the next day. The one plane which we had available, we spent most of the night trying to camouflage it on the ramp. The one which was definitely out was put over as far as we could over to one side on the ramp and left it out for bait or whatever.

After we had launched all of the planes, we were looking at it and it looked exactly like a PBY sitting in the middle of a junk heap. So we decided that maybe it would be best to get it out of the way. I got elected to head the rescue thing.

Massie Hughes told me to fly down to Laysan or Lisianski and fly around down there until they told me to come back and pick them up. Well, as we were about to do that, we got the word that our planes had sighted many planes inbound to Midway at some hundred miles out. So takeoff became an emergency situation, as far as we were concerned. We did have gas in the plane, but among other things that had been cannibalized in this plane or were inoperative was at least one of the electric starters. So somehow or other, we didn't have the hand crank, but somebody ran over to the other plane and got a hand crank out of that one and they were cranking that up as it was going down the ramp and as soon as it caught, I must have blown the guy off the top of the wing as soon as the beaching gear was off. By starting my takeoff right from the ramp, I was just going over the southern end of the atoll when the Japanese were coming in the northern end. Well, I went out and they recalled me somewhere around noon. I was under the impression that we were keeping Pearl Harbor time, but that doesn't seem to agree with the timing of other things. In other words, this was somewhere between halfway from the time we got up in the morning and the time it would have gotten dark at night. So I speak of it in that sense.

Again, we were certainly under the impression that accompanying the carriers were a number of battleships and we were expecting them at 12 o'clock. Not having heard anything differently, they could have very well have been getting close to within range. So again, takeoff became somewhat of an emergency exercise. The only thing about it this time that we needed, certainly, was a reasonable amount of gasoline, maybe another 500 or 600 or 700 gallons to get back to Pearl Harbor. This had to come out of drums without any pump of any kind, so a bucket brigade was formed, and you've never seen buckets produce 500 or 600 gallons of gasoline so fast. We opened up a plate on the top of the tank so that it could be thrown in a whole bucketful at a time, and somewhere we found the buckets; I don't know where. But we got out. My memory was that we had 25 people aboard that night, which I thought was a record because that meant that they were standing in the aisles more or less until I heard that Tom Moorer had exceeded me again and somewhere down in one of their evacuation moves in the Dutch East Indies, had taken off 29 people along with four 500-pound bombs which he refused to dispense with because he thought he might be able to use them on the way somewhere.

Q: So you were the pilot of the getaway plane?

Capt. O.: Yes. Again, this raises a question that you mentioned a little while ago of what was I at that stage of the game. I seem to think that I was the Flight Officer. Maybe I was the second senior; I don't know. I know that we had lost our regular exec, as I said before. But none of my records show any particular duty. I presume I was the second senior, but I was still functioning more as a flight officer than as an executive officer. Massie Hughes had been in the command post with Simard during most of that time out there, which is why I didn't believe that Ramsey had been there as you told me the book by Lord had indicated.* But I do know

---

*Captain Cyril T. Simard, USN, Commander of Midway atoll.

that during the time that I was out standing-by, Massie was in the command post.

Q: But you did not make any of the patrol search flights yourself?

Capt. O.: Yes, my recollection is that I had conducted the search on the day we expected to find something and didn't (2 June).

Q: How was the rotation figured on who would fly a particular day?

Capt. O.: Well, in actuality, what we did was go out there with 12 planes and everybody flew because we were flying every plane that we had. The only thing that changed any situation like that were the two planes which didn't take off. So obviously, when Massie didn't fly, there was another plane commander in any case, that was available to take his normal plane out on search. I'm sure that Thueson, who was one of those that made contacts that morning (Ensign Thueson who was one of our ex-APs), was in the plane that I would normally have flown. He had flown with me on the day that I did go out. Of course we had no record-keeping capability out there which is why it was a question as to what entries I have in my log for that period. The dates are all mixed up, so it's concocted basically from memory some time later and I'm sure that they're not as accurate as they might be.

Q: Was there a rotation on who would fly? You just did it when your turn came up for making these patrols?

Capt. O.: No, like I say we had 12 planes and 12 crews. So everybody flew. The only difference would be that when we got down to ten planes, we were searching $90°$, and that meant we would have a $9°$

sector. It would be only the number of sectors that we would use. If we had all 12 planes, we would fly a narrower sector which would give us a better coverage.

Q: I guess what I'm trying to get at is why you flew the first day when they were expected and not the day when they were found.

Capt. O.: I presume that because Massie had directed me to stay there and on the morning we were sure that things were going to happen, he wanted me to be there. He intended to be in the command post most of the time, so he wanted me in charge down at the ramp.

Q: I see.

Capt. O.: That is the way I would assume it would be. If we had had 12 operational planes, I'm sure I would have gone out, since I had done so on the day before where we might have made contact.

Q: You mentioned that one of the reasons you thought your squadron went out was because of the radar. Did it prove to be useful in this instance?

Capt. O.: Let's say I don't think it was. The reason is that on the day before the attack, if we were going to find them at the extreme range, that would have been the day and we did not find them. If they were there, the radar didn't find them. When flying 700 miles out on a $9°$ sector, there was about 100 miles across out there. Since that radar's range was much less than that, there's no way you could tell if the radar was good. We didn't find them with radar.

This evacuation flight that we made, we took off just ahead of the Japanese planes incoming and flew around until about noon and came back, did our emergency gassing and piled in all of the crews that we had on hand there from the two planes and whatever maintenance people we had including the skipper, Massie Hughes, and flew back to Pearl. My records show that we knew that the planes were scattered. I presume that the VP-44 planes came back in and landed after their search and some of ours must have, but some didn't because they were floating around in several different parts of the ocean afterwards.

We got back into Pearl well into the night on the 4th. We came back out to Midway on the 7th with what planes had gotten back to Pearl and what else we could pick up one way or another and I know we had roughly 12 planes out there conducting a search for the survivors. We picked up, as I recall, some 17 pilots, mostly from the carrier planes, including Gay, the lone survivor of Torpedo Squadron 8.* VP-44 had the only plane loss. They had one plane shot down, not by carrier planes but by a battleship or cruiser-based seaplane. This plane went out of control and somehow or another, at least five people ended up being thrown out through the sides of the plane and, as I understand it, one of them was very severely wounded with his whole stomach split open. They survived for five days before we picked them up, including this fellow in a life raft with some holes in it so that all the blood was draining out and attracting the sharks. It was an absolutely amazing rescue.

---

*Ensign George Gay, USNR.

When we came to Pearl, I presume I was the exec. It wasn't very long after our return from Midway on the 27th of June until the first week of July our squadron was beefed up to 15 planes. I don't know where they came from, but we were given 15 planes. We didn't get the pilots to go along with them, to the best of my knowledge, so all the crews came from our squadron. This means that under normal circumstances we would have 15 crews available but probably no more than that. As soon as these 15 planes were ready to go, we were ordered, on temporary duty, to proceed to the South Pacific, with me as acting commanding officer.

Q: At what point did you become the Acting CO?

Capt. O.: Well, when we departed.

Q: Do you have a date on that?

Capt. O.: Yes. My orders were dated the 7th of July, 1942. My flight log shows that the first flight was conducted on the 8th of July from Pearl Harbor to Palmyra, on the 9th from Palmyra to Canton, on the 11th from Canton to Tonga. On the 14th, we went from Tonga to Suva. The reason for this three-day delay--and I'll explain what the problem was later--was that we couldn't get any weather at Tonga to get to Auckland. On the 15th from Suva to Auckland and on the 16th from Auckland to Noumea. My orders for this expedition were "When directed you will proceed by naval aircraft to places in reference A. This is in addition to your present duties.." and so forth and so forth. "The confidential nature of this travel is such that the stops cannot be revealed in this order." This is labeled "Travel Orders." I terminate these orders with my return on the 13th of October and have written down here two sets of itineraries that encompass the whole period of time that we were down south. I have one other notation in here that I was designated the CO of Patrol Squadron 23: "Detached Patrol Squadron 23, proceed report combat duty involving flying as Commanding Officer of Patrol Squadron 23." That was dated 8/23/42.

Q: How did you find out where to go? Were you given your orders...

Capt. O.: I was given verbal orders. Incidentally, this was in reference to a ComTaskForce 9 dispatch of high classification. In other words, the particular transportation that was involved here was Kelly Turner and several senior members of his staff which I was transport to Auckland, New Zealand.*

Q: Where did this whole journey start? At Pearl?

Capt. O.: At Pearl, yes.

Q: Did he ride in your plane?

Capt. O.: Yes.

Q: Well, tell me more.

Capt. O.: Really there's not that much to tell. With a senior character like that aboard, I wanted to make sure that everything went as well as possible, so I tried to stay in the seat as much

---

*Rear Admiral Richmond Kelly Turner, USN, was going to the South Pacific to command the Guadalcanal invasion force.

as possible and when we got where we were going, everybody was pooped enough that they took to their own quarters. Obviously Kelly had lots of things to talk over with the people in the staff that was with him, so I was just a chauffeur as far as that goes. I didn't have that much conversation with the admiral.

Q: Did you form any impressions of him during that period?

Capt. O.: No, not really. I barely knew of him by reputation. One of his Marines I did talk with, "Cootie" Weir who was a Marine aviator.* So we had some fly talk. But basically, as I say, we were just providing transportation and I didn't have much more contact with him than I did with Admiral Byrd on the way down to the Antarctic.

Q: Did you know what was coming off, that this was with Guadalcanal?

Capt. O.: Yes, we knew exactly what he was going down there for and what the urgency of the situation was because as you know, the Guadalcanal operation did start on the 7th or 8th of August, just a month later from the day we took off.

Q: Had this information also come to you from the patrol wing headquarters?

Capt. O.: The real purpose of beefing us up to 15 planes and taking a whole squadron down rather than just...I say my three planes only flew into Auckland. The rest of the 12 planes went to Suva direct and then from there to Noumea where the Curtiss was. So I was several

---

*Lieutenant Colonel Frank E. Weir, USMC, Assistant Operations Officer (Air).

days later than that getting my three planes up to the Curtiss. So when I did arrive at Noumea, I relieved Squadron VP-72 and VP-14. This occurred over a period of time, a week or so. Then I got six planes from VP-11. I found out later that I had thought that those six planes were assigned to me all the time. Recently I have talked with my classmate Joe Cobb who was the operations officer of VP-11 at that time. He said that the assignment was not a continuous one but rotational from their squadron which was based over in Fiji. So we always had six planes from VP-11, but not always the same six. The six planes from VP-24 and six from VP-51 were in essence a part of my group because they were not an organized division. They were planes and plane crews with no maintenance or support people at all.

Q: So you essentially had operational control of them.

Capt. O.: This was something that I still haven't been able to understand--exactly why we departed from a standard procedure. Normally, when planes are based aboard a tender or a carrier of any kind, they come under the complete operational and administrative control of the tender or the ship commander. In this case, I functione more as a task force point something, point something, point something working directly under Admiral McCain and his chief of staff Captain Matt Gardner, on the Curtiss and not reporting through or taking orders from the skipper of the ship. I would see him from time to time and mostly have breakfast with him, perhaps, and keep him updated on what was going on, but as I remember it, I worked directly under the admiral himself and not through any patrol wing group, but merely as senior squadron commander, there being no other squadron commander present.

Q: So you were essentially the patrol wing commander.

Capt. O.: In essence, with 33 airplanes. It was pretty good for a senior grade lieutenant.

Q: And Admiral McCain's position then was Commander Aircraft South Pacific?

Capt. O.: Yes, that's correct. While talking about the command structure, or lack thereof, it is interesting to see how I received my orders to return to Pearl after replacement squadrons had arrived. First there is a memorandum signed by "M.B. Gardner, Chief of Staff" and addressed originally to me and to Commander Paschal[*] (the CO of one of the replacement squadrons) but with these names scratched out and "CO Curtiss" substituted in longhand. This memo specifies that a particular plane (flyable but not suitable for patrol) be made ready for return to Pearl; that I was to take this plane with a minimum crew of my choice; and that Major James Roosevelt, USMC, would be a passenger. Another paragraph states that Commander Patrol Wing 1 should give me orders to report to ComPatWing 2 at Kaneohe. Two days later I received quite proper orders from ComPatWing 1 informing me that my temporary duty with PatWing 1 was completed and to go on home. This was signed by H.S.

---

*Commander Joe Bennett Paschal, USN.

Kendall. The peculiar thing about all this is that I did not then know anything at all about the existence of such a command in the South Pacific area. I did not report to it on my arrival there; I received no orders of instructions from it while there; I did not report my departure to it; and, to the best of my knowledge, I never met H. S. Kendall.

Q: What were your recollections of Jim Roosevelt?

Capt. O.: Well, he was helpful and very nice and a very gracious passenger. He had come from a very strenuous operation with Carlson's Raiders, so he was much more of a combat veteran than I was, in the real sense of the word. His major's leaves were properly cruddy, whereas mine were bright and shiny, but he always addressed me as "Skipper," and he was just as pleasant and as nice as he could be. His presence assured the two of us of good treatment when we went through.

Q: This was before he and Carlson went on the Makin raid, wasn't it?

Capt. O.: No, it must have been after because he was coming back, he had been detached from the Raiders. I'm not familiar with the dates on that, but I'm pretty sure that he wasn't just going back to Washington on temporary duty or something. I was under the impression that he had been detached.

Q: Did he discuss his experiences at all then?

Ogden #2 -88

Capt. O.: No. I don't know. There again, we were a little bit shorthanded on this plane going back, and I was doing most of the flying. The only time I remember him was the night we spent in Canton at a Pan Am hotel which was like a 1940 motel, if you know what that represents. But they did have a little radio that could get KOA Denver, and his dad was making one of his fireside chats the night that we were there. We sat around the radio with the Pan Am people and enjoyed the fireside chats commentary with son James.

Q: What sort of things was he saying?

Capt. O.: I don't remember and I wouldn't dare quote him if I did. It was just comments like, "That sounds like Dad."

Q: Could you describe how much contact you had with Admiral McCain in your relationship with him?

Capt. O.: Well, of course, I say that I was classmates with John Sidney McCain. He was one of the senior officers that were given a quick course of sprouts in flying so that they would qualify for command posts. With the advent of all the carriers and so forth, we realized we didn't have aviators from the ground up with enough seniority to handle the jobs, so there were quite a number of people at that stage, very senior captains, that were expected to perform these functions and I understand McCain did quite well over this whole period of time. But down in Pensacola, I had the distinction of having his left leg when he was thrown in the bay after his solo flight, which is about the extent of his flight career. He soloed after telling his instructor, "Son, the Bureau of Navigation sent me down here to learn to fly. Now, you do it." He used to sit around down at the beach and chat with the students that were in Squadron 1 in Pensacola. He was a self-proclaimed weather prophet because his rheumatism acted up, and he could tell two days in advance when it was going to rain. He had false teeth. He was at the stage of the game when they were a little bit loose, and he would sit down there and clack his teeth. He was a lot of fun to be around. It was sort of a little vacation for him and he was real friendly. I saw him daily while we were down at Espiritu Santo while I was on the Curtiss. I guess I worked with Gardner more than with McCain, but basically both of them. It was a small staff, and I don't remember anybody under the two of them that much except one of my classmates who was a supply officer on the staff. But McCain was quite reasonable to work with. He and I had some differences later after he had come back and was in Washington somewhere and I was down in Pensacola and he sent me a memorandum saying that he was disappointed the patrol plane people in the South Pacific had not gotten any individual awards for their work down there and would I please look through my records and see if I couldn't make some recommendations. In all fairness, I had to say that I had made some recommendations while I was down there and was under the assumption that he had sent them on to higher headquarters or the Awards Board or whatever for final action, but that I was completely unable to find any kind of records that we had kept down there because in essence I had no administrative people to handle things like that. I find myself having referred in some of this correspondence to a VP-23 log, but I don't remember having kept it. We did get one administrative officer down somewhat later in the proceedings, but he left and was detached from the squadron down there and never came back to Pearl. I was never able to get in touch with him, so unfortunately, those people down there never did get any special recognition as far as I know, other than the gratis air medals that were put up for numbers of flights in enemy territory.

Q: Could you describe some of those flights, please? The ones you made.

Capt. O.: Well, let me think. The Curtiss moved up to Espiritu Santo from Noumea in the first week of August. The landings in Guadalcanal were due to take place on the 7th or 8th of August, as I remember. Shortly after we got to Espiritu, we were looking for some place to base some planes a little bit closer to the operational area that we were to cover after the landings had taken place. We picked an island, a little atoll, Ndeni, as an advance base that would be handled by one of the two small tenders that we had, the Mackinac which was the first of the AVPs that I had seen, the first one down in that area to be involved with, and the McFarland, which was a converted four-stack destroyer that we had had in Patrol Wing 1 in San Diego. The McFarland didn't do very much tending because mainly she was carrying gasoline for the planes that were at Guadalcanal. So the Mackinac got the job.

At Espiritu, in addition to our PBYs, was a group of about the same number of B-17s under the command of "Blackie" Saunders.* Because these planes had the firepower to fight off the land-based fighters in the area, they drew the patrols "up the slot." With that exception, our planes were responsible for patrolling the sector from west around northeast out to a range of 700-800 miles.

You asked about some of the flights that we had. As things developed, I kept noticing one particular search sector--with everything supposed to be the same length, a plane would come back almost an hour later than everybody else and I finally got somebody to tell me what it was. It seems that this sector went over Stewart Island. Most of the inhabitants on the islands in this area were Micronesian or Melanesian--rather unattractive black types. The ones right around us were cannibalistic. As a matter of fact, while they were working to build a field at Espiritu, they tried to enlist some labor from Malekula, the next island down. The chief down there said, "We come by and by. Right now we just raided tribe and we have Kai-Kai long pig for the next few days."

But Stewart Island was inhabited by Polynesians, brown skin types, and it seems that the maidens in the villages would go out fishing in the shallows and when our planes came by they would wave and the only things they had to wave were their sarongs. So the pilots would somehow or other manage to go back and forth a little bit extra in their search than they would have otherwise.

Q: Did they fly lower after some of their searches?

---

*Colonel LaVerne G. Saunders, USAAF, Commander 11th Bombardment Group (H).

Capt. O.: I'm sure they flew at their minimum altitude. Incidentall there was a carrier affray in that area during the time we were there, and one torpedo pilot managed to get in his life raft and got ashore on this island. He delayed at least a week in signalling our people that he was available for rescue. A little R and R in the middle of the war, I guess.

Q: What did you see in the way of Japanese during your flights?

Capt. O.: Well, we had some good and some bad. I think my squadron undoubtedly has a record of being the only PBY squadron that ever shot down an enemy plane. One of our crews came across a Japanese seaplane and fortunately, was above it with some broken clouds and spotted it before they spotted us. They made one pass at it and got a splash.

Q: With a .50-caliber?

Capt. O.: Yes, I'm sure it was a .50-caliber, although the kind of approach he had to have made, the bow gun, one of the .30-calibers would have had a shot. One one occasion when we ran across somethin the pilot made an erroneous report--of reporting cruisers as carriers--which caused the evacuation of Espiritu Santo. The boss didn't take too kindly to that. Unfortunately, the next day when I needed one extra crew I had to pick one to repeat so I sent him out. The only word that we got from him was "Being attacked by enemy aircraft," and he never showed up again. We lost one other crew a little bit later with no word at all. The radio down there was very, very peculiar in that you would get skip distances and you could hear all kinds of things going on back in the States, but you couldn't hear the planes that you wanted. We had to shift frequencies quite a bit in order to get through reports when we had them. We had one plane--and I believe it was one of the planes from the other squadron--that was attacked, as I understand it, by six carrier fighters and in their melee, he ran them all out of ammunition and escaped. At least they broke off and went home or something. I think they lost one man on board. It was the radioman, I believe, that was shot. The plane had some holes in it which we managed to fix all right.

The Mackinac received a visit one day from some of our carrier planes who, as I was, were not that familiar with this as a new type of ship for us, so they left a couple of 500-pound calling cards which killed the chief steward's mate, which was a great loss. It also made the skipper extremely jittery, and after the planes had taken off in the morning, he would put the rest of the crews in the boats and then go over the horizon and wait until the evening to come back home and take care of the people. This made it pretty hard on these crews who were, at this stage of the game, flying like you couldn't believe. One crew I know, with my friend Norm Brady as plane commander, (who comes up later in my story), flew over 250 hours in the month of August*. This is as much as the whole squadron could fly in a month in a period of time not too long before Pearl Harbor.

---

*Lieutenant (junior grade) Norman K. Brady, A-V(N) USNR
 (Later Captain, USN).

One other plane that ran into trouble, a plane from VP-51 this time, with plane commander Clark, was shot up while out on a course to the north-northwest. They knocked out one engine and they put a lot of holes in the plane and a few holes in some of the plane crew, including one guy who had a hole right through his stomach and they put corks in both ends and filled him up with sulfa. The plane flew on one engine almost 200 miles, as I understa it, and landed in Ontong Java Atoll, which was still within our search pattern. But it was also in the search pattern for the Japanese planes, so everyone there were a little bit touchy about attracting too much attention. They were entertained royally by the king of this island and were doing all right, but it was a littl while, a few days, before they finally managed to flag down one of our planes and were brought back. As luck would have it, the day after we got back, Clark himself ended up with an emergency appendectomy that would have been fatal if he hadn't been back by then.

One little episode, again, brings up an operational first as far as the participants are concerned and possibly even as far as PBYs or any other Navy planes might have been. One night they had decided that we should have three planes to be at the extreme end of our search pattern up the slot at nightfall to look for the Tokyo Express possibly coming down. Norm Brady and two other pilots were selected for this mission, so when they returned--which was obviously towards midnight or in that area--we were down to a 300-foot ceiling and visibility none too good below that. With a peak on Espiritu roughly 8,000 feet, or something like that within a few miles of where we were and directly between the planes and ourselves, and other mountains around, I gave them their choice of landing in the open sea while they could see what was going on (that is, to land with their flares giving them light to land), or that I would try to bring them in. Well, the other two elected to land at sea and made it all right. They took off the next morning and came in, although they were uncomfortably close to the islands--more than they thought they were. But Norm said he would let me try to bring him in. This was before we had such things as CIC, and the very rudimentary air search radar was in one room of the flag area of the Curtiss with the radio in another room and the chart room in another. So by getting him up at a comfortable altitude above the mountains we brought him over until we could pick him up on radar. I got bearing and distance from the radar room, ran into the chart room to plot his position, and ran into the radio room to tell him what to do. I got him to come into an open area to the eastward and circle down, moving in or out as need be to keep him out in an open area until he got down and broke through below the clouds. Then we had all the search lights turned on the two ships that were in there and he came in and made a landing. So as far as I know, it was certainly an original GCA landing, if not the first.

Q: GCA stands for ground control approach?

Capt. O.: Ground control approach. I didn't get very many flights because, as I've said, I was not only the senior squadron commander,

I was the only squadron commander and from there on down, since even I was a senior grade lieutenant, there was sparse pickings in terms of experience. So whether by edict from McCain or just realizing that was the way it was, I did not do much flying. But one night we were ordered to send three planes to Guadalcanal with torpedoes for a night attack on the Tokyo Express if it came. (It was the only real hairy flight I had in this area.) With the only experience in the group with torpedoes, I did take on the lead of this group and the most reliable pilots I could find for the others. This was a bad night for weather. I got to thinking, as time went on and I started to get close (incidentally, we tried to go up in formation but couldn't make it because of the weather and got separated), but I was beginning to have feelings like I did coming back into Pearl the night of the 7th as to how many people on the ground at Guadalcanal knew I was coming and what for. I was wondering who I was going to have the most trouble with--the Japanese or the Marines. I don't know who was informed of what we were coming for, but certainly I could not contact anyone on the radio, so it became obvious from the weather and everything else that this wasn't going to gel, so we turned around and came back. It was interesting and I have wondered just what would have happened if we had run into them. Apparently the Express didn't come on schedule that night.

That's about it on that aspect of the thing. One point I think needs to be told about and that is the logistics and the maintenance problems that we encountered, since as I say, we were able to bring down only the plane crews plus some few specialists from the squadron maintenance office and no administrative at all. The Curtiss air department was not that well stocked with parts and certainly not prepared to take care of that many planes for that period of time without getting some degree of augmentation from outside which apparently wasn't forthcoming because there wasn't all that much surface traffic going on. The air traffic was basically the PB2Y run that would come down and stop by once in a while and drop off some mail. One time they made the mistake of bringing some official mail and I never even opened the bag; I just turned around and put it right back on the plane and said, "Take it back and leave it at Pearl. I'll read it when I get back." But our crews were excellent, and they did a marvelous job. The Curtiss could take one plane aboard at a time to make major repairs. When I say major repairs, the harbor of Espiritu Santo was not always as smooth as it might be and we would pop rivets in the hull from the rough water. The only thing that kept us going in this respect was a big supply of pencils for the navigation desk ostensibly, which was fortunately provided with a pencil sharpener. So every time we popped a rivet that we could tell about, we put this sharpened pencil in and would break it off and sharpen the pencil again and get ready for the next one. When we couldn't catch them, the water would leak in or sometimes would come in around it or we tried to pull them out when we'd land. Anyway, the next morning, if the water was over the floor boards, it was time to bring it aboard the Curtiss and drain it out and plug up the things. So this came pretty close to being an operation like the barnacles down in San Juan. It was funny to see these planes when they took off in the mornings looking a little like a porcupine on his back. When they pulled the pencils out, there would be a stream of water coming down until the plane was off in the distance.

Q: What was the mood at Guadalcanal when you were patrolling in that vicinity?

Capt. O.: Well, very obviously things were tight on the beach at Guadalcanal, but our problems were sufficient to keep us on our toes because in spite of the fact that we only lost two crews and had some narrow escapes with others, the PBY was a flying turkey as far as running into enemy ships was concerned. We knew they were out there, because we had seen them and you could expect them out there in the day. When you go out every day wondering whether you're going to come back and you haven't had rest and you've been flying more--I broached this subject to my friend Jack Smith on the golf course the other day, he being a flight surgeon, and said, "What would you have done if you had been told that a pilot had flown 250 hours a month?"

He said, "I would have grounded him long before he got to that point, as not being ready to keep on flying and do his job properly." So along with the living conditions that they were up against and the fact that the airplanes were so long overdue for major overhauls, the engines and planes themselves, we were becoming, in my estimation, not only ineffective, but that the results of this would be such that some of these people would not be of value to us later in the war because they would have just been completely--mentally and physically and emotionally--shot from being exposed to this over this period of time.

Q: Did you express this concern to Admiral McCain?

Capt. O.: I wrote this to my boss at home suggesting that. I showed it to McCain. He didn't endorse it one way or the other. He said that was something between me and ComPatWing 2. I don't think he liked it very much, but I felt I had to do it.

Q: But he was still giving the orders on how many...

Capt. O.: I was not questioning him about the job we had to do. I was making a plea, to Commander Patrol Wing 2, to send somebody else down to relieve us from this temporary duty that we had been sent on which was beginning to look much more permanent than we had expected. I felt that there might be other planes that could share in the thing, because we couldn't do the job much longer.

Q: Do you think that letter prompted, then, somebody else coming in to relieve you?

Capt. O.: Yes, I think it also prompted the fact that I was ordered back before the rest of the squadron was, too. But that's by the by. It's funny that I had to be writing that letter to Mitscher after what I had told you about his looking after the crews back when he was Patrol Wing 1 and told Adolphus Andrews where to get off. But I didn't mention that to Mitscher when I got back.

Q: Did he seem annoyed that you had written?

Capt. O.: He didn't tell me so and I've never seen my fitness report but I'm almost positive that it was not all that well received. But so be it.

What I just said about the effect on the squadron--I think we should go back and sort of look at the situation that we were in from about mid-1940 until the 7th of December 1941 in terms of our patrol missions and examine what we might have been able to do and what the effect of it would have been as compared to the patrol mission that our squadron had at Midway and the mission that my group had at Espiritu Santo in the Guadalcanal area.

I believe that already I have remarked that the problem before Pearl Harbor was something that the patrol plane couldn't have made that much difference with because you had to know what the threat was going to be. If you decided that the threat was going to be a carrier attack, as it ended up to be, unless we had some fairly specific information or ideas of when it might occur, the only warning that we could give by a full 700-mile search was in the order of a half a day--that we would find them at noon one day and they would attack at dawn the next morning. If you found them and got your message off and somebody believed it, you could get your ships away from an anchorage, but you couldn't get anybody there that wasn't there to begin with. You could alert everybody, but if you started that patrol in June of 1940, after 18 months, you wouldn't have any patrol planes available to fly that mission at the latter part of that. We would have run out of gasoline, we would have run out of money, we would have run out of planes and the crews would have been exhausted. In addition the replacement crews would not have been trained at all.

If you tried to make some halfway measures like a 300-mile antisubmarine patrol and you had an air attack, that wouldn't guarantee you that you would get any more than, at the most, an hour's notice. And if that attack came on a Sunday morning, you wouldn't even have time, unless everybody was on standby, you wouldn't be able to get more than a portion of your airplanes in the air and none of the ships out of the harbor. So, I think that the answer then that you would see from that is that this--even with the assumption that a 700-mile search around $220°$ would give you positive ability to find a force out there (which is dubious)-- it wouldn't give you enough warning on the face of it to do much more than call people to general quarters a little bit earlier.

Q: Well, that would have helped.

Capt. O.: Yes, it might have.

Q: But I think you're saying that you would have had to pay an unacceptable price in order to achieve that.

Capt. O.: I'm sure of it. But now let's look at the situation that Midway represents. The battle of Midway was basically won in the basement of a building in Pearl Harbor by the 15th of May because regardless of exactly how the information developed, it gave us time by the 15th to recall the three carriers from the South Pacific, to get them to Pearl, to get the Yorktown fixed and to get all three ships in position to do something about it. By having some very specific information as to where we might expect to find so-and-so and so-and-so, it terms of the exact composition of the ships and the fact that they were two separate forces makes all the difference in the world.

Q: Were you told the source of this information?

Capt. O.: No, I didn't know. But the information was specific. If it was a ruse, by the Japanese, that was something that they always had to consider, but they took that chance.

Q: I know there was great security given to these intercepted translated Japanese messages, and I wonder how much detail they went into with, say, the patrol plane pilots on where they got this information.

Capt. O.: Nobody told me where the information came from. But it was so specific that you didn't need three guesses to figure it out. I think I was more thoroughly briefed than the Japanese pilots were, because at least I knew where our people were going to be, which was more than they did, and I knew where all of them were going to be.

But let's see a vision of what might have happened at Midway had it not been quite that specific, only that it was going to happen at Midway. Well, without knowing that the striking force was going to be to the northwest and the landing force was going to be to the southwest, we go out there not sure of the date, perhaps. We go out there as soon as we can and start flying like mad. This was about the maximum of the patrol planes that we could put on those islands without their sinking. One squadron was all that they could handle with the one ramp that we had in our place and there were B-17s and augmented Marines and everything else on the landing field. So this was all we could do. On the 3rd, we would have found a group of ships to the southwest. But nothing to the northwest. The ships that were sighted were primarily transports but it was some time before it was determined that this force did not contain the carriers and warships which could be expected in such a situation. Any immediate reaction to this threat would have put us far out of position to counter the real threat--the striking force which our patrol had missed because of weather. So, our patrol plane operation at Midway was not, in a sense, a search, but rather a verification of previous information which was just astoundingly accurate. Had we gone out to Midway with anything less than the total information we had or the forces it enabled us to assemble, relying on our best search for timely information, the battle would have had a decidedly different result.

With the experiences of VP-23 at Midway and in the South Pacific as a background, it would be interesting to reexamine the problems of whether we should, or indeed could, have run a 700-mile, $200°$ search out of Pearl during any substantial part of the period from mid-1940 to December 1941. The classic test for a military plan is threefold: Is it feasible? Is it acceptable? And is it effective?

Feasible--can we carry it out with the resources available? Given the political and budgetary climate of the U.S. at this time it is virtually impossible to imagine that the Navy could have provided the money, fuel, people, plane replacement, and overhaul for an operation at least ten times greater than that actually conducted. Be assured it would have required such an effort.

Acceptable--can we afford to accept the losses to be expected? Our experience in the South Pacific convinces me that the two operations would have been proportionally equivalent. In this case, when war came we would not have had patrol forces adequate to support current war plans.*

Effective--if the plan succeeds, would it accomplish the desire results? We have seen that at Midway only timely and precise intelligence gave us the chance to win--time to gather our forces and enough specifics to enable our commanders to correctly evaluate the search results. Only by having warning that a major portion of the Japanese fleet had left home waters and the resultant alert of our fleet would have justified an all-out search effort. Otherwis the warning given by search alone (if any) would have been of minimal benefit.

I think that the direction of the whole war in the Pacific was much, much better (it became a carrier war) because it was run by a combination of people who either had aviation experience or who were as adaptable as Spruance and Burke and people of that caliber who showed they could get out of the fixed idea of how things had been done since Lord Nelson was running the show.

---

*Richardson, Why Were We Caught Napping At Pearl Harbor?

Q: After you were detached from the patrol planes following the Guadalcanal experience, what did you do then?

Capt. O.: I was ordered down to Pensacola. They had nothing in particular ready for me when I got there, but after a month of messing around with one thing and another, I relieved a classmate of mine Joe Phillips,* as the commanding officer of VN-3D8 as the Pensacola Instrument Squadron. This squadron was the only one that I know of at Pensacola that processed all of the students going through Pensacola regardless of what their specialties were going to be. We were teaching a new idea in instrument flying which had been developed, I believe, primarily by Henry Bridgers, who I have mentioned as being in the squadron with me at Patrol Wing 1, and another Buster Pound. Between the two of them, they had come up with a much more realistic idea of how to teach instrument flying.

When I had gone through flight training and during my early application with flight training, we flew our instruments. That is, if the needle (which was a gyro control thing) went to the right, we would push our foot on the left rudder and that would make the needle come back to the middle. Then they had a ball in a liquid in a semicircular tube and if it got off to the right, it meant presumably that the right wing was down, so we'd bring the right wing up and the ball would come back up in the middle. You could keep this up for awhile, but eventually it got to be terrific and then vertigo would take over. It was not a comfortable way to fly.

---

*John L. Phillips, Jr., USN, who was lost in the Truk raid of February 1944.

For one thing, we had a new instrument--a gyro horizon--in which you had a picture of a little plane and a horizon. Then these people developed the idea that we should have flight <u>through</u> instruments. In other words, we looked at the instruments not to tell us what mechanical thing to do, but to visualize what was happening to the airplane. Then the needle in the ball took on a completely different aspect, exactly opposite to what we had been doing. The needle, as it went to the right or left, showed us that what was happening was that we were turning because one wing was down. It was only by banking that you got enough aerodynamic force to bring you around in a turn. When the ball went off, it was because the plane was in an unstable condition. In other words, we were slipping or skidding. So we used the rudder to balance the plane and then the ball returned to center. We looked at this needle, ball and air speed along with the gyro horizon, and we were trained to see what the plane was doing and then you flew the plane just exactly as if you had gotten that same information from looking outside the cockpit. This was producing such good results for these young students that unfortunately from that time on, they found it much easier to fly that way and so they were flying around looking into the cockpit and were flying around running into each other when they got to the other squadrons. Our squadron didn't lose very many students, but others were.

Q: Was it difficult for you to make the adjustment, having learned the old system?

Capt. O.: When I knew I was coming to this squadron, I went through the first part of the procedure and I had about four flights and then they gave me a check and somehow or other, they had come up with a bonus situation so that the mark that I had was a 4.32 on a scale of 4.0. So that's how hard it was to catch on. It certainly paid off in terms of all the later flying that I did in transports and other types of flying. It was all the difference in the world--you could fly just as long on instruments and just as comfortably on instruments as you could looking outside, and a great deal more precisely.

Q: Were there any other highlights from that period of Pensacola?

Capt. O.: Other than the tremendous students, flight hours and everything else which can be appended to this account.

Q: Then you had gotten sort of into the patrol plane regime because of your extended tour at the beginning of the war. Did this eliminate you from going back into other types of planes as had been the prewar custom?

Capt. O.: No, but my experience did more or less dictate that I was an appropriate candidate for a tender. In early 1945, I was ordered to commission the Floyds Bay (AVP-40). After shake-down training we headed for Okinawa where the fleet was at that time.

Q: Could you recount a little about what went on in the shipyard? This was a fairly new experience--obviously your first ship of your own. How did you make the transition from being a plane man to a ship man?

Capt. O.: Of course I had qualified as officer of the deck under way on my first ship (the Chicago). Then I had two more years on the Northampton right out of Pensacola. All the time we were aboard ship, I stood duties. I even stood deck watches on the Oglala going down to Palmyra one time. The Floyds Bay was really very easy to handle, and I only made a couple of boo-boos, but I also once in a while did some things right. I had one beautiful experience in Wakayama [Japan] right after the war. I had a couple of old destroyer skippers on board who had just been relieved and were headed for home and waiting for the PBM to come in so to take them to Yokosuka.* It was a rainy day with no planes flying. I decided to go alongside the tanker and take on fuel because I had to shut down my radios while that was going on and we couldn't have planes flying around and not be able to use our radios. So these destroyer skippers were licking their chops watching an aviator make a mess of himself. So we got under way and I had to make a sharp turn to get to the tanker lying anchored nearby. I went through the whole operation and finally, coming right alongside, everything looked just right and I backed down once, stopped all engines and they were talking about throwing the lines over to the tanker and I said to hold off. Finally we came up right alongside and stopped right dead at the place we were supposed to be and didn't even bump into the ship. They handed the lines across and I said, "That's it. Secure the special sea detail. Let's go down below and have a cup of coffee." These guys' eyes were popping out--and so were mine, as a matter of fact.

---

*PBM was the Navy's Martin Mariner seaplane.

Q: I bet they were disappointed.

Capt. O.: It was a real nice ship. It was awful rough at sea, because it came pretty close to having a bottom like an icebreaker and you know what that means; it rolls around. My neighbor had command of a Coast Guard type and he confirmed my belief that this wasn't the most pleasant thing to take through a typhoon, which I had done a couple of times.

Q: How much experience did you have tending planes when you were commanding officer of that ship?

Capt. O.: Virtually none at all during the war. In Okinawa, I went into Chimu Wan and there were either two or three of the larger tenders of the Curtiss type and a couple of ours. There were not quite as many planes as they usually had because there had been a typhoon where they had gotten caught there and had lost a whole bunch of them. But we actually did tend a group; we would help with the refueling and that sort of thing, but rarely during that stage or even later during the process did we really have a group actually based on board. There would be a little bit at a time. But after the war, we were in various places as a station ship and with PBM crews running a courier service. They had one base in Hokkaido and Yokosuka. I went into Wakayama first, which is at the eastern entrance to the inland sea. We would have gone into Kobe but there were mine fields there that we thought we knew where ours were and the Japs thought they knew where theirs were, but nobody really knew where any of them were and so we were a little reluctant to go in there. We went from there to Nagoya [Japan] and from Nagoya to Shanghai [China] and from Shanghai to Tsingtao and back to Shanghai and back to Tsingtao [China] and into Sasebo [Japan]. There were also stations at Hong Kong and at Saipan. We were just a floating hotel and service station boat for planes flying through. It was interesting to me because from the air, I got a look at Hiroshima practically before the dust settled when we first got there and I went through Nagasaki on land.

Q: Did you have any contact with the Japanese during this period?

Capt. O.: Yes. I didn't get to do much personally, because I was the only aviator aboard and with these planes, I was acting as tower controller at the same time and I couldn't be gone too much unless there were no planes coming in that day or the weather was bad or something like that. But the Japanese were very docile. I think the report that came from the group that I went in with to evacuate the prisoners of war (which we never ended up doing because they didn't bother to come down there; they just got on a train and went to Tokyo), but as we were going in, the boss of the outfit was on a cruiser and as they started through this entrance to the Inland Sea, they saw on the hills on either side these coastal guns, big guns, and the admiral remarked to the Japanese pilot, "Boy, you've really got us where you want us if you want to start shooting now."

The Japanese pilot was reported to have said, "You make joke. We're happier this way than you are." So they were very glad to have it over; they were very deferential. As a matter of fact, they were much better than the Chinese. We could leave our stuff around and leave buoys in there and go off and come back three months later and they'd still be right there. In Tsingtao, I laid out six buoys with a 500-pound anchor and a 100 feet of inch and a quarter steel wire on this buoy in the afternoon and a boat went around to inspect the planes at 8:00 o'clock at night, and all six of them were gone. I don't know how they got them, but they used to make shoe soles out of the rubber. Since we had already lost some, we had chains around the buoy part itself and welded it together and welded all the shackles to the anchor and everything else all together. They just took the whole thing.

Q: In daylight, too.

Capt. O.: With only an hour and a half of darkness. In Nagoya we had a very important decision. I did have six planes there, and we got word that a typhoon was coming from down around the Okinawa vicinity. It was predicted to go by, and we weren't going to get too much wind, but enough that we wanted to get all the planes out of there. Unfortunately, the wind came up faster than expected and we had to send the planes down to Saipan, because there wasn't any other place that they wouldn't run through the stuff on the way through. But one plane couldn't get off and it damaged the hull a little bit. So we put it out to a buoy and unfortunately I made a decision that we would try to put a skeleton crew aboard that night to try to see if they could ride it out at the buoy. Unfortunately, the dog-gone typhoon went right straight smack-dab over our heads. We lost one man of the crew and the whole harbor was a mess of ships dragging anchor all over the place. The hospital ship was going all over the place itself. We got caught there and decided we shouldn't go to sea because they had a whole bunch of LSTs and all the minesweepers and everything else.* It was just a great big mess.

Q: Where did you go from there? When did that tour wind up?

Capt. O.: That wound up in July 1946, so we were out there a year after the war ended. Then I was ordered back to the Philippine Sea, which had been commissioned after the war and then, due to a shortage of people, had been put in virtually a caretaker status before it had gone on its shakedown cruise.** The navigator was a classmate of mine who was aboard but all of a sudden, they had a casualty or something and needed a navigator for one of the other carriers. So they took him off and I was ordered to report as navigator.

Q: Were you a commander by this time?

Capt. O.: Yes, I had made commander down in Pensacola.

Q: So you were an aviator who was having his first carrier duty as a commander.

Capt. O.: Yes.

---

*LSTs were tank landing ships.
**USS Philippine Sea (CV-47)

Q: Which is unusual.

Capt. O.: Yes, that's right. I got stuck with the big boats. Very shortly after I got to the Philippine Sea, they did bring our crew up to battery, so we went down to shakedown training in Guantanamo and were recalled a little early from that to go on Operation Highjump. So we came back and were in Boston yard getting fixed up and trying to get stuff aboard. (Those details were taken care of in this book you showed me).*

I do remember that in December of that year I see in my orders that I was ordered down to the hydrographic office to pick up what information I could on antarctic piloting. I made it a personal thing to try to go in and see Byrd** and talk to him about what problems I might encounter. Well, I had an appointment with Byrd, but I found out somewhat less than anything about my problem. He seemed to be very vague and he was not particularly helpful. My wife was living with her mother at Prince George Street here, right across the street from Weems Navigation School, so I was able to get much more information and help and material from Weems than I did from him.*** Because we were going to have helicopters aboard (as I remember, from the first group of five helicopters that were available for shipboard use). I was thinking that by picking up a bubble octant that sometime I would get this guy to take me up above an overcast and see if I could get some sights, whereas otherwise I might not. Very fortunately, I didn't go out

---

* Lisle A. Rose, Assault on Eternity: Richard E. Byrd and the Exploration of Antarctica, 1946-47 (Annapolis: Naval Institute Press, 1980).
** Rear Admiral Richard E. Byrd, USN.
*** Captain Philip V. Weems, USN (Ret.).

on the first trip they made because that's the one that lasted 27 seconds from takeoff to landing alongside in the water. They mentioned in the book that we had several on board. As far as I know, that was the only one. So that removed that source of navigation. On the trip down, as far as the navigator was concerned I got awful tired the further down we got going through the South Pacific, having the evening star sights at about 10:00 o'clock at night and the morning star sights at 2:00 o'clock in the morning. So I fortunately found that I could do very well because the sun and Venus were in the proper positions and I could get them both in the daytime and I could get my noon position from that. So there was no problem with navigation on the way down. Incidentally, the transit through the [Panama] Canal was also an unusual propsect- not on the way down, but in anticiaption of coming back. One side of each set of locks was out of commission because they had never done any work on it after the wartime era, so they were doing much-needed repairs. As a carrier went through the canal in those days (which it could), you would always put your starboard side, which was flush, all the way up to the center wall because the buildings, the block houses (control towers) along the center wall between the two locks were very close to the side. Something would always be knocked off a block house every time a carrier would go through. They'd take out something along that center wall. But you'd go on the left hand side of the road, a la British, you know, putting your starboard side to the wall. We did that all right going down, but coming back we were going to put our portside, where you have all of your overhang, to the wall. This meant that on the way down, we had to stop at the Coco Solo side and have them chop off some of the outer parts of our gun tubs and then after we came back through the other side, we had to paste them back on again before we went home.

Q: So there was no thought of going through backwards?

Capt. O.: No. This was an exercise that the pilots in the canal took very seriously. They have sort of a mock-up that they can work the thing through and they worked on that thing all the time we were down south. It takes five master pilots to go in through anyway. They have one in each of the four corners of the flight deck and then the pilot, in addition, has a platform built up from the flag bridge out to the centerline of the ship so he can sight right down the center line. They got us through on the way back without any strain.

We got down to the Ross Sea and made our rendezvous. As we approached the area where we expected to encounter ice, we wanted to have the helicopter scout ahead before dusk because we did not know how bergs would show up on radar. That's when we lost the copter. We found out what an iceberg looked like anyway. Incidentally, they were absolutely amazing. The icebergs in that area are really quite different from those in the Arctic, their size in particular. There are two different kinds. One is a flat type that breaks off from the Ross Ice Shelf and goes to sea and (it's been reported that they've seen them as much as 100 miles long). The biggest that we saw was only about 10 miles long, and abou

300 feet high. They are just pure white when the sun is shining. This one in particular, waves had scooped out arch-like recesses in its side and you could see the reflection in there of water with a bluish and greenish glow. It was really magnificent. The other type were tall and irregular. I measured one that was sticking up 1,500 feet. This solved one of my navigational problems, by the way. We had found an open area near the pack ice and were just milling around waiting for suitable weather, both where we were and also in Little America. The winds were variable. A carrier is like a big sailing ship when that happens, so there was little way to keep track of where we were. So I broke out something that Byrd didn't tell me--the Antarctic pilot--and found that in that area there was a very constant one-knot current. I figured that these icebergs would respond to these currents and not to the wind for obvious reasons. So we just picked out one and called her "Myrtle." I kept situation on Myrtle for six days and ended up, when I got my next sight, a quarter of a mile off my DR.*

Q: That's great. So you were plotting the DR of the iceberg.

Capt. O.: I was plotting the DR of the iceberg. The rendezvous which we had was with one ship from each of the three groups on Highjump plus the Sennet**. The icebreaker Northwind was from the Central Group and the tanker Cacapon from the Western Group and then the destroyer Brownson that had come over with the survivor of the PBM that had crashed from Pine Island, Howard Caldwell's

---

*DR - dead reckoning navigational plot
** USS Sennet (SS-408).

experience down there.* Incidentally, it's Howard Caldwell who is referred to as "Henry" in the book. But this transfer, as far as the destroyer and getting the people, that wasn't much of a problem. When the icebreaker came alongside, we were doing a highline transfer of material that we had brought down to each of these groups that they hadn't been able to pick up before they left. They had left quite a bit before we had. The icebreaker was rolling and we had to make about eight knots because of the little bit of swell. The little bit of swell was making that icebreaker look like it was riding out a hurricane and the people over there were calling over to our people, saying "How do you like the shore duty?" But the big problem was going along with the tanker alongside, because with a ship of that size and a ship of our size being together, you have to make course changes only about a degree or so at a time. This got to be a little touchy because during the period of transfer, CIC reported that they had counted at one time 109 icebergs on the radar screen at the same time. So we were threading our way in and out with one-degree changes and hoping that we would miss all of these things.

The return to Balboa, because of the casualties we had aboard from the plane crash, was at 25 knots. We had not refueled from the tanker because they were anxious to save their fuel for the ships that they were tending. We went all the way from Panama, 6,500 miles down to the Antarctic at about 20 knots and all the way back at 25 knots without refueling for 13,000 miles. We were

---

* Captain Henry Howard Caldwell, USN, commanding officer of the seaplane tender <u>Pine Island</u>.

practically on fumes when we got in. I don't know that anybody has tried to run a ship like that quite that far without a refueling.

Q: Did you have any contact with Admiral Byrd during the cruise?

Capt. O.: No, not really. He kept very much to himself in flag quarters. I was in the position on the bridge to see the dispatches that were going, so I knew the exchanges that he was having with Cruzen down under, and I can certainly verify that there was a conviction on both sides that there were two different people running that operation and neither one of them was prepared to admit that the other one...there was a bit of tension.* No, he rarely showed up. He certainly didn't. I don't know that he would have anyway. I didn't feel that I had to ask him for help with the navigation, although I'm sure he had the run of the ship. No, there was practically no contact at all. I saw him two or three times.

Q: Well, after your experience in Washington, you probably wouldn't have wanted to get too much help from him.

Capt. O.: He didn't turn me off that much; it's just that he didn't seem that he was that much interested. So I wasn't trying to push it.

Q: It sounds as if he was not very outgoing during this cruise.

---

* Captain Richard H. Cruzen, USN, commander of Operation Highjump.

Capt. O.: He had things on his mind. He was concerned, I'm sure, and perhaps a little upset that he was being used more or less as a figurehead, and it was not his operation, really. And I seem to agree with the write-up in the book to that extent.

Q: Any other interesting experiences during your time in the Philippine Sea?

Capt. O.: No, not really. From there on out, I had a rather usual career. I had a little bit of everything, two and a half years in BuAir; on the staff of the Atlantic Division Military Air Transport Service [MATS], I was naval representative and did some flying with one of our transport squadrons right after the Berlin airlift. As a matter of fact, while MATS was getting involved with the Korean airlift out in the other direction.

Q: What was the role of a naval officer in an Air Force organization?

Capt. O.: Well, because the Atlantic Division of MATS of course had a lot of Air Force squadrons, they also had attached to it VR-6, which had 12 R5Ds (C-54, DC-4).* We were on the Atlantic run. I'll show you where our stations were and where in one way or another we operated. I made a trip around the horn with the commanding general one time that went through Port Lyautey, Morocco, Tripoli, Libya, Cairo. We even went over and had breakfast in Dhahran, Saudi Arabia which was the end of our line and the beginning of the one going on from there into the Pacific on the trip around

---

* VR-6: Navy Transport Squadron 6; R5Ds: Navy Skymaster transports (Navy version of C-54).

the world, back to Nicosia, then to Athens, from Athens to Ankara, Ankara to Athens, Athens to Rome, Rome to Paris, Paris to Wiesbaden, Wiesbaden to Berlin. We didn't have a station in Berlin, but planes did run there from Frankfurt, then over to England, Scotland and back to Keflavik, Iceland, and Stevensville, Newfoundland.

Q: Sounds like you got around.

Capt. O.: All of that was in a 17-day trip.

Q: Who was the general that you were with?

Capt. O.: One of the finest gentlemen I've ever run into and one of the finest officers--I keep calling him an admiral because he's good enough to be an admiral--Jimmy Spry, James Spry, a general, a West Pointer and a real, real gentleman.* We had a lot of fun together and he played a pretty good game of golf. He wasn't quite as good as I was at the time.

Then I went to the Naval War College and was a student with the same class with my old friend Tom Moorer, he keeps cropping up all the time. And incidentally, also Jimmy Roosevelt was there for a while, not for the whole class, but he came in for a Reserve seminar or something like that. I went to the Armed Forces College for two years on the faculty, as Chief of Staff of Carrier Division 15, ASW group. We were first on the Point Cruz for one deployment to WestPac and then I went aboard the Boxer and went out to Pearl and ran fleet exercises up there for an antisubmarine problem out

---

*Major General James W. Spry, USAF, Commanding General, Atlantic Division, MATS.

there before being detached and was sent back to OP-54, the training section in OpNav.

Q: Who was the Admiral when you were on the carrier division staff?

Capt. O.: Practically all of it was Bill Nation, who incidentally was one of the original pilots of the PB2Ys that I talked about.* As a matter of fact, his name is in my flight log. One time he came out before the war and took several of us out just for an indoctrination flight and we went to Kaneohe for practice landings. So I had run into him before.

Q: Is there anything you remember about him in this tour in the carriers? Any interesting experiences?

Capt. O.: Nothing really. Of course, the operations of the ASW people were, again, a completely new and different thing than on the Philippine Sea, where the little bit of work we actually had during the shakedown and some of the later stuff, was regular carrier operations. There were fighters, and it was interesting that I got a chance to fly after all my years, just to get my time in. They let me get up and fly one of those damn things which was over a small field not all that long and had a 40-foot cliff on one end of the thing, so you had better know how to land. I was wondering whether I was going to make it with this thing. With those airplanes, all you had to do to land is just cut the gun and you're going to land. You'd better be in the right place to do it, that's all.

---

*Rear Admiral William M. Nation, USN.

Q: It sounds like you could use the arresting wires on the field, too.

Capt. O.: But with CarDiv 15 we were working with the helicopters and had quite an interesting deployment in that this was practically the whole ASW training schedule for all of the destroyers in the Pacific and they were really going to get working with an ASW group. We had a division of antisubmarine destroyers which stayed with us all the time. Then we would get four or six destroyers, from the groups out there and run this exercise. I managed, I think, to convince the submarine people who worked with us that we were interested in training and not in having a contest which they could win hands down when the sea was rough and we could win hands down when the sea was calm. So we would adjust and play the game so it was about as realistic as we could make it. It was quite an interesting thing.

The big exercise we had out in Hawaii was really interesting. It was sort of a fictitious problem, but it was one that brought in just about everything, and we even used some submarines on our side as a deep sonar long-range search. The submarine was not designed for that purpose as some of them eventually got to be, but it worked well enough so that he was able to pick up--the thing was rigged so that the guy had to snorkel sometime, because he was trying to get somewhere on schedule--the enemy--for missile launch, so they picked him up snorkeling at quite a distance away-- 50 or 60 miles or something like that. We made contact on that. The whole thing was really quite interesting.

Q: This was about the time that Rear Admiral Jimmy Thach was getting quite a bit of acclaim for ASW work.* Did you encounter him in your duties?

Capt. O.: No, we were playing this strictly by ear and just trying to see what we could do. On the East Coast, I think they had come up with an experimental group to run that.

Q: This is the one Thach had.

Capt. O.: Well, yes. That was while I was at the Armed Forces College, that I think that was being formed there. But out on the West Coast, there were just two of these CarDivs and one of them was out all the time and then would come back and go out again. The Point Cruz, when we took it out, was one of the jeep carriers on a tanker hull and surprisingly, made a good platform for the type of planes that we had -- the S2F and the helicopters. The Philippine Sea was more comfortable.

Q: I'm sure it was.

Capt. O.: But the Boxer, that was nice.

My last real tour of duty was out at Taiwan, and it was interesting because of the people that I ran into. It didn't turn out quite the way it was supposed to be. I was sent out to be chief of staff of the MAAG.** The MAAG and the Commander of the Taiwan Defense Command were supposed to merge. After a tentative

---

*Rear Admiral John S. Thach, USN.
** Military Assistance Advisory Group.

start in that direction, MAAG (which is Army controlled) decided that in spite of the fact that the Joint Chiefs of Staff had approved of the merger, that they disapproved of it. Somehow or other they got their way, and I ended up being Deputy Chief of Staff on the Taiwan Defense Command with not very much of anything to do. We did have some interesting times out there. While we were there, they were doing some shooting around the offshore island in August of 1959, I guess, and everybody was really wondering whether it was going to turn out to be a full-fledged war or not. I remember making the remark to somebody, "I don't know about it now, but I will certainly know by the 9th of September if there will be a war or not." On the 7th of September, Curtis LeMay was coming out there and was going to meet with "Tiger" Wong and if the two of them could get together for two days and can't start a war, you can't start one.* Tiger Wong was the Commander of the Chinese Air Force at the time and Curtis LeMay needs no introduction.

Q: Right.

Capt. O.: But they were two of a kind. Tiger was a real Tiger and was not misnamed, although a delightful character. I ran into him, as a matter of fact, in the Superintendent's house over here at the Academy when he was here and Tom Moorer was taking over as CNO and they had the ceremony over here. Draper Kauffman, a classmate of mine was the superintendent and I had lunch at the table with Tiger and he remembered me in our doings out there.

---

* General Curtis E. LeMay, USAF, then Air Force Vice Chief of Staff.

I got Chiang Kai-shek's* picture with his personal chop on it down addressed to Navy Colonel Ogden in Chinese. I have a translation. Admiral Liang, the Navy Chief from way back and another Huang who was the Chief Logistician whose emblem was the three-humped camel. The three humps stand for carrying of the supplies to the three -- the Army, the Navy and the Air Force. General Pung, the army commander, looked like a little kewpie doll. After he had entertained us at the Grand Hotel [in Taipei] one evening (he had just Betty and myself for dinner), Betty was just captivated by him and I tried to tell her that he was the same guy who lined up 10,000 Taiwanese in the race track one time and shot them all. She still doesn't believe me, but I've been assured the story is true.

Q: That was quite a race track story.

Capt. O.: Old Admiral Liang was a funny one. He was from one of the western provinces noted for liking all their food highly seasoned with garlic and everything else, so every time he would talk, he would always cover his mouth up with his hand. He had a very charming wife, a good bit taller than he was, but very shy. Most of these people spoke English. When they were making a speech, they would always have a translator and he was a wonderful guy, too -- S. K. Hu. S. K. Hu and his wife both graduated from Michigan and they spoke some vernacular English. I'm sure that he always gave a speech that was a damn sight better than the one that the guy was giving in Chinese.

---

*Chiang Kai-shek, President of Taiwan.

But to get back to Admiral Liang, somebody at a party remarked "Mrs. Liang doesn't speak much English does she?" The admiral replied "No, she doesn't speak much Chinese, either."

That was a delightful tour out there and we had a lot of personal contacts and a lot of sightseeing and acquisitions, as you can see here. We wouldn't have missed meeting them for the world. It's a nice way to wind up a Navy career.

Summary of Training, Naval Air Training Command,
Pensacola, Florida--8 April 1943 to 6 April 1944

Students

On Board at Start	Received	Failures	To Other Duty	On Board at End
712	13,583	112*	12,730	1,453

Instructors

225	532		325	432

Training Planes

160		248

Flying Days

Scheduled	Lost Because of Weather	Flown
363	70	292

Flight Hours

Students	Total
251,013	262,679

*Failures included 8 as a result of flight checks; 90 dropped at their own request; 3 killed during training; and 11 for miscellaneous reasons.

INDEX

CAPTAIN JAMES R. OGDEN

Ady, Lieutenant Howard P., Jr., USN (USNA, 1939)
  Patrol plane pilot in VP-23 who was in principal search
  sector during Battle of Midway and later became executive
  officer of squadron, p. 46.

Andrews, Vice Admiral Adolphus, USN (USNA, 1901)
  As Commander Scouting Force during fleet exercise in 1938,
  gave order for patrol planes commanded by Marc Mitscher to
  remain on station despite fog--an order ignored by Mitscher,
  pp. 12-14.

Antarctica
  Explored by U.S. Navy's Operation Highjump in 1946-47, during which Ogden was navigator of flagship Philippine Sea,
  pp. 113-19; description of icebergs, pp. 115-16.

Antisubmarine Warfare (ASW)
  ASW Patrols by PBYs before Japanese attack on Pearl Harbor,
  pp. 42-3, 47; unorthodox patrol for Japanese midget submarines immediately after attack, p. 68; training exercises
  conducted by ASW group in Pacific while Ogden was chief of
  staff for ComCarDiv 15, 1955-1957, pp. 120-23.

Avocet, USS (AVP-4)
  Small seaplane tender used as base for patrol plane operations west of Hawaii before World War II, p. 30.

B-26s
  U.S. Army Air Forces bombers whose crews were given torpedo
  training at Pearl Harbor in early 1942, pp. 72-3.

Barnacles
  Infested PBY patrol planes at San Juan, Puerto Rico, in
  1938 because of high sewage content of water; had to be
  scraped off before planes could fly, p. 17.

Boxer, USS (CVS-21)
  Flagship of Carrier Division 15, involved in ASW exercises
  in the Pacific in mid-1950s, pp. 120-23.

Brady, Lieutenant (junior grade) Norman K., A-V(N), USNR
  As member of squadron VP-23 in August, 1942, flew PBYs an
  astounding 250-plus hours during the month, p. 93; involved
  in one of first radar ground-controlled approaches while
  flying patrol in the Solomons in 1942, pp. 94-5.

Bridgers, Lieutenant Commander Henry C., USN
  As aviation cadet at Pensacola in late 1930s, p. 8; work
  on instrument training at Pensacola and writing of instrument training manual in 1943-44, pp. 8, 105.

Byrd, Rear Admiral Richard E., Jr., USN (USNA, 1912)
  As head of Operation Highjump expedition to Antarctica in
  1946-47, an aloof figure, pp. 113, 118-19.

California, USS (BB-44)
    Battleship attacked at Pearl Harbor in 1941; bomb intended for her landed in naval hospital on Ford Island instead, pp. 67-8.

Carrier Division 15
    U.S. antisubmarine warfare group built around USS Philippine Sea, conducted exercises in Pacific in mid-1950s, pp. 120-23.

Cobb, Lieutenant James O. ("Joe"), USN (USNA, 1933)
    Relates story about Japanese attack on Kaneohe NAS in December of 1941, p. 61; as operations officer of VP-11 in 1942, p. 85.

Coco Solo Naval Air Station, Panama Canal Zone
    Intermediate landing site for mass flight of Navy PBY patrol planes in early 1939, pp. 15-6.

Collins, Captain James R., Jr., USAAF
    Army B-26 pilot briefed on torpedo operations by Ogden at Pearl Harbor in early 1942, pp. 72-3.

Cruzen, Captain Richard H., USN (USNA, 1920)
    As commander of task force involved in Operation Highjump exploration of Antarctica in 1946-47, had uneasy relationship with Rear Admiral Richard E. Byrd, p. 118.

Curtiss, USS (AV-4)
    Seaplane tender based at Noumea and Espiritu Santo while serving as Rear Admiral John S. McCain's flagship during Guadalcanal campaign in 1942, pp. 84-90, 97-8; involved in early radar controlled approach of PBY during poor visibility in 1942, pp. 94-5.

Enlisted pilots (Aviation Cadet Program)
    First class trained in 1938; hurriedly commissioned after the attack on Pearl Harbor, pp. 7-8, 28-9, 32.

Enterprise, USS (CV-6)
    Aircraft carrier spotted from air by PBY pilot Ogden when he was making flight in wake of Japanese attack on Pearl Harbor, pp. 54-8; Enterprise planes shot down when approaching Ford Island, p. 60.

Espiritu Santo
    Island in the New Hebrides group in South Pacific used as U.S. patrol plane base during Guadalcanal campaign in 1942, pp. 89-97.

F4B-4
  Navy fighter plane flown in tight formation at night by Ogden and Thomas Moorer at Pensacola in late 1930s, p. 24.

Fleet Problem XX
  U.S. naval exercise in the Caribbean in early 1939 involving Captain Marc Mitscher's tactical training of PBYs in formation bombing, pp. 17-9.

Flight training
  Improvement of instrument training devices in 1943-44, pp. 8, 105-07; summary of training statistics for the period from April, 1943 to April, 1944, p. 127.

Floyds Bay, USS (AVP-40)
  Small seaplane tender which Ogden put into commission in early 1945, then commanded off Okinawa right at the end of World War II, pp. 107-10.

Guadalcanal
  Squadron commanding officer's observations on PBY support of Guadalcanal campaign from Noumea and Espiritu Santo in the summer and fall of 1942, pp. 90-8.

Hanson, Lieutenant Murray, USN (USNA, 1933)
  PBY pilot whose plane landed in dry lake bed in Texas in 1941, pp. 21-2.

Hughes, Lieutenant Commander Francis Massie, USN (USNA, 1923)
  As commanding officer of squadron VP-23, accompanied Ogden in first PBY which took off from Pearl Harbor during the Japanese attack in 1941, pp. 51-7; activities in connection with the Battle of Midway in June of 1942, pp. 77-81.

Instruments-Flight
  Much improved method for training students in use of flight instruments developed for pilots at Pensacola around 1943, pp. 8, 105-07.

Intelligence
  Quality of information before the battle of Midway, pp. 39, 76-7, 101-02; peacetime reconnaissance around Pearl Harbor, p. 32; lack of information before the attack on Pearl Harbor in 1941, pp. 34, 36-7, 57, 100-01.

J2F Duck
  Amphibious biplane, among the first U.S. aircraft to launch from Pearl Harbor after the Japanese attack in December, 1941, p. 54.

Japanese
  Loyalty to the United States of those with dual citizenship during World War II, pp. 57-8, 69.

Japanese vessels
  Midget submarines reported off the coast of Hawaii prior to the attack on Pearl Harbor, pp. 34, 68.

Liang, Admiral Yuen-li
  Former Taiwanese Chief of Naval Staff whom Ogden got to know while serving in Taiwan in the late 1950s, pp. 125-26.

Mackinac, USS (AVP-13)
  Small U.S. seaplane tender which established base at Ndeni in Santa Cruz Islands in summer of 1942 and was mistakenly attacked by U.S. carrier planes, pp. 90, 93.

Mauna Loa
  Hawaiian volcano which Ogden observed from the air around 1940 when fountains of lava were flowing down the sides, p. 32.

McCain, Admiral John S., USN (USNA, 1906)
  As flight student at Pensacola in the mid-1930's, pp. 7, 88-9; as commander of aircraft in the South Pacific during World War II, pp. 85-6, 89.

McDonald, Lieutenant David L., USN (USNA, 1928)
  Future Chief of Naval Operations as training squadron flight officer at Pensacola in the late 1930s who reprimanded an overzealous instructor, p. 24.

Midway Island
  Living conditions during 1942, pp. 73-5; intelligence before battle in June of 1942, pp. 39, 76-7; preparation for battle by PBY squadrons stationed there, pp. 76-80; Ogden's thoughts on possible outcome of the battle if prior intelligence had not been available, pp. 102-03.

Mitscher, Captain Marc A. (USNA, 1910)
  As commanding officer of Patrol Wing 1 in 1938 ignored an order from VADM Adolphus Andrews during an exercise in deference to his pilots' safety, pp. 12-4.

Moorer, Admiral Thomas H. (USNA, 1933)
  Experiences as a pilot before and during World War II, pp. 1-2, 8, 24, 49-50, 78; relationship with Ogden, pp. 23-5, 27-8, 63, 120, 124; at Pearl Harbor during attack in December of 1941, pp. 49-50, 61; with squadron in Dutch East Indies in early 1942, pp. 70, 78; family, pp. 23-7, 62.

Nation, Rear Admiral William M., USN (USNA, 1927)
  Commanding officer of Carrier Division 15 in the mid-1950s who had previously helped to indoctrinate Ogden in then-new PB2Ys, p. 121.

Navigation
  In PBYs, pp. 10-11; aboard Philippine Sea (CV-47) during Operation Highjump in 1947, p. 116.

Nevada, USS (BB-36)
  Battleship beached by Japanese attack at Pearl Harbor that posed a hazard to planes attempting to land in channel by Ford Island because she blocked approach lights, p. 59.

Ogden, Captain James R., USN (USNA, 1933)
  Family, pp. 23-7, 62, 66, 69, 113; duty on cruiser Chicago (CA-29) 1933-35, p. 9; flight training at Pensacola, 1935-36, pp. 7-8; duty with aviation unit aboard cruiser Northampton (CA-26), 1936-38, pp. 9, 108; as member of VP-7 of Patrol Wing 1 in 1938-39, pp. 6-23; duty in VP-23 of Patrol Wing 2 from 1939-42, pp. 15, 27-62, 64-104; at Pearl Harbor during attack in December of 1941, pp. 47-62; at Midway Island during action in June of 1942, pp. 76-81; commanding officer of instrument squadron at Pensacola, 1943-44, pp. 105-07; commanding officer of seaplane tender Floyds Bay (AVP-40), 1945-46, pp. 107-112; duty aboard carrier Philippine Sea (CV-47) during Operation Highjump in 1947, pp. 112-19; on staff of Atlantic Division, Military Air Transportation Service (MATS), from 1950-52, pp. 119-20.

PBY Catalina
  Characteristics, pp. 1-6, 20-2, 32, 37-8; manning and duties, pp. 20-5; navigation ability, pp. 10-1; bomb, torpedo, and other training prior to World War II, pp. 14-5, 18-9, 31-8, 42-3, 44-5, 47; antisubmarine patrols before Japanese attack on Pearl Harbor, pp. 42-3, 47; at Pearl Harbor during attack, pp. 50-60; immediately after Japanese attack, pp. 64, 66-7, 70; during Battle of Midway, pp. 76-81; rescue patrol after Battle of Midway, pp. 81-2; during Guadalcanal campaign in 1942, pp. 41-2, 54, 84, 90-8; losses, pp. 50-1, 70, 81, 92-3, 98.

PBY-5 Catalina
  Newer model PBY received by Ogden's squadron just prior to the Japanese attack on Pearl Harbor; had a slight modification to make it more combat efficient, pp. 37-8.

PBY-5A Catalina
  Up-dated PBY-5 with retractable landing gear to make an amphibious version; pooled at air station in Hawaii after attack on Pearl Harbor, pp. 70-1, 73.

PB2Y Coronado
　Four-engine version of the PBYs that were sent to Pearl Harbor from San Diego after the Japanese attack to replace lost aircraft, p. 70.

Pearl Harbor, Hawaii
　Conditions in the late 1930s, pp. 26, 30; pre-World War II PBY operations, pp. 30-47; attack by Japanese aircraft on 7 December 1941, pp. 47-62; atmosphere following attack and conditions, pp. 64-5, 67-9; Ogden's thoughts on U.S. preparedness for Japanese attack, pp. 35-6, 100-01, 103-04.

Philippine Sea, USS (CV-47)
　Carrier receives one of first group of shipboard helicopters in 1946, pp. 113-14; unusual transit of Panama Canal in 1946, pp. 113-41; flagship of RADM Byrd during Operation Highjump in 1947, pp. 115-18.

Point Cruz, USS (CVE-119)
　Escort carrier used temporarily as flagship of Carrier Division 15 in the mid-1950s, pp. 120, 123.

Radar
　PBY's in Ogden's squadron among first aircraft to be equipped with radar, just prior to Battle of Midway, p. 71; lack of value in locating approaching Japanese fleet in June of 1942, p. 80; one of the first radar ground-controlled approaches (GCA) made by a PBY after a patrol in the Solomons in 1942, pp. 94-5.

Ramsey, Lieutenant Commander Logan C., USN (USNA, 1919)
　Operations officer in Patrol Wing 2 at the time of the Japanese attack on Pearl Harbor who drew up search plan used by first planes aloft; plan originally intended to locate Japanese subs reported off Hawaiian coast, pp. 52, 78.

Roosevelt, Major James, USMCR
　President Roosevelt's son who was a passenger in Ogden's plane after detaching from Carlson's Raiders in the Pacific in 1942, pp. 86-8.

Sanders, Lieutenant (junior grade) Eddie R., USN (USNA, 1930)
　Flight instructor at Pensacola reprimanded by David L. McDonald after a training flight with Ogden and Thomas Moorer, p. 24.

Saunders, Colonel LaVerne G., USAAF
　Commanded group of B-17s in support of Navy's PBY patrol around Espiritu Santo during Guadalcanal campaign in 1942, p. 91.

Turner, Rear Admiral Richmond K., USN (USNA, 1908)
  Flown by Ogden from Pearl Harbor to Auckland, New Zealand
  in July of 1942 to command the impending Guadalcanal
  campaign, pp. 83-4.

VP-7 (Patrol Squadron 7)
  Personnel, pp. 7-8; operational exercises and training on
  the West Coast in 1938, pp. 10-15; torpedo practice in
  1938, p. 14; mass PBY flight from San Diego to Coco Solo
  to San Juan in early 1939, pp. 15-7; operational exercises
  including night bombing practice on the East Coast in 1939,
  pp. 17-9.

VP-23 (Patrol Squadron 23)
  Personnel in 1939-1942, pp. 28-9, 33, 46, 51-2, 57, 93-4;
  basing and maintenance of PBYs at Pearl Harbor before
  World War II, pp. 30-1; pre-War operations, pp. 31-4,
  36-7, 40, 43-7; during attack on Pearl Harbor, pp. 50-60;
  operations between attack on Pearl Harbor and squadron
  transit to Midway Island in May, 1942, pp. 64, 66; basing
  at Midway before battle, pp. 73-6; during Battle of Midway,
  pp. 46, 76-81; patrol search for survivors of Midway attack,
  pp. 81-2; during Guadalcanal campaign of mid-1942, pp. 41,
  54, 84, 90-9.

VP-44 (Patrol Squadron 44)
  Assigned to Sand Island in the Midways equipped with PBY-
  5As in May of 1942, p. 73; sighted Japanese force approaching Midway on 3 June 1942, p. 76; plane loss during the
  Battle of Midway, p. 81.

Winters, Lieutenant Commander Robert C., USN (USNA, 1927)
  Executive officer of VP-23 who was killed in a plane crash
  of a PB2Y in May of 1942, pp. 28, 70.

Wright, USS (AV-1)
  Converted lighter-than-air aircraft tender used during most
  of World War II as a seaplane tender with only marginal
  efficiency, pp. 6, 16-7, 20; supported VP-7 on mass non-
  stop flight of PBYs from San Diego to Coco Solo, Canal
  Zone, and then on to San Juan, Puerto Rico in January of
  1939, pp. 15-7.